THE IF THAT CHANGES EVERYTHING

What if you could believe that Jesus rose from the dead?

The If That Changes Everything

Published by:
The Good Book Company

thegoodbook.com | thegoodbook.co.uk
thegoodbook.com.au | thegoodbook.co.nz

Every book published by The Good Book Company has been written by a human author and edited by a human editor. While AI tools are sometimes used to assist with research and support certain processes, all content has been created by a human author and thoroughly checked by our editorial team.

Cover design by Drew McCall

ISBN: 9781802543742 | JOB-008513 | Printed in India

"How can one weekend change everything for everyone? Mike Hood doesn't just show you how; he shows you why—and the profound difference Easter makes. This book will give you solid reasons not only to believe in the resurrection of Jesus but, even more, to love it."

GLEN SCRIVENER, Author, *The Air We Breathe*

"I highly recommend this helpful and inviting book. Mike Hood covers not only why believing in the resurrection is rational but also why it's beautiful—why it makes life worth living. His language is accessible, readable and sympathetic, but never simplistic or patronizing. He draws on plenty of real-life examples of people who have wrestled with belief in the resurrection. I would recommend this book both to those who already believe (but need to remember why it matters) and to those seeking answers to the big questions."

TED TURNAU, Author, *Popologetics*

"This book combines a compelling, concise demonstration of the evidence for the resurrection with a unique emphasis on the relationship Christians have with the living God and with one another. A stunning combination! This book will be my go-to giveaway. It's short, warm and convincing."

LINDA ALLCOCK, Author, *Deeper Still*;
Ministry Leader, The Globe Church, Central London

"A great short introduction to the case for the resurrection of Jesus. Without the resurrection, things don't make sense, but this book shows that when we accept the truth of Jesus' resurrection, it makes the most sense of the historical evidence and of life itself."

DR PETER J. WILLIAMS,
Principal, Tyndale House, Cambridge

"In a world of shifting questions and beliefs, Mike Hood offers something solid: a clear, compelling case for why the resurrection of Jesus isn't only credible but life-changing, and even world-changing. Mike doesn't just explain why the resurrection is a believable fact of history; he shows why that fact is so good. To read this book is to hear an invitation to explore how the resurrection of Jesus makes sense of history, shapes our identity and offers genuine hope. Whether you're exploring faith or looking to deepen it, this is a book worth reading."

MATT LILLICRAP, CEO, UCCF

"The question of whether Jesus rose from the dead is, as Mike Hood so clearly shows, the most important question we could ask. This is a brilliant guide for the curious that not only unpacks why we *can* believe it but also why we *should*. The resurrection of Jesus is not just a historical reality—it changes everything!"

MICHAEL OTS, Author and apologist

"Ace communicator Mike Hood distils the case for the resurrection of Jesus in clear, persuasive and readable prose. A great book to share with a friend to start a conversation about—arguably—the central event in human history!"

STEPHEN C. MEYER, Author, *Darwin's Doubt*

CONTENTS

INTRODUCTION

"Did you know that if you eat a whole cabbage, you will die?"

I don't think this question was on the school chemistry syllabus, but Mr Mavrommatis was easily bored. So in a dull moment he had wandered up to one of my classmates and asked her this alarming question.

She was incredulous. "No way! That can't be true, can it?"

Before long the whole class had been drawn into the debate: "Surely not, sir! That can't be right! If cabbages were poisonous, someone would have warned us before now!"

But he insisted: "I promise you it's the truth. If you eat a whole cabbage, you will die."

Eventually, after he had soaked up an enjoyable amount of teenage scepticism, Mr Mavrommatis paused for a moment and grinned at us through his bushy beard.

"Okay, look. I never said *when* you would die."

We looked at him, nonplussed.

"If you eat a whole cabbage, you will die. And if you don't eat a whole cabbage, you will die. Everybody dies, kids."

Why do I still remember that joke nearly two decades later? I think it stuck with me because it's so rare for anyone to say it out loud. "Everybody dies." It's the most basic fact of human existence, something we all have in common. Yet it's also something we don't like to talk about. Mostly we try not to even *think* about it.

We tend to assume that thinking about death would drain all the colour out of life—so we cram it into a dusty cupboard at the back of our minds, shove the door shut, and brace ourselves for the day it comes bursting back out at us. But what if the truth about death could actually fill our lives with meaning and hope?

I'm convinced that it can.

Why? Because I'm convinced that Jesus rose from the dead.

The If That Changes Everything

You probably know the Easter story. Jesus Christ, the central figure in the Christian faith, was put on trial before Roman and Jewish authorities in the 30s AD. On what we now call Good Friday, he was unjustly executed on a cross. But that Sunday, Jesus came back to life. His tomb was found empty, and he appeared bodily to many different people for six weeks—eating with them, embracing them, and explaining to them what it all meant, before finally returning to heaven.

If that's true, it changes everything.

It revolutionises our perspective on life after death. It means we aren't stuck with vague hopes about "going to a better place"—hopes that start to fall apart if we look at them too closely. Instead, we have a solid reason to believe that death is not the end. Jesus has come out the other side of it into a life that he says will last for ever—a life that is joyful and personal—and he offers us that future too.

But that's not all. If this is true, it would also transform life *before* death. It might not seem obvious yet, but the more you think about Jesus' resurrection, the more you'll realise how huge the implications are. If Jesus rose from the dead, then he really was who he said he was: our Creator, who became a flesh-and-blood human being to introduce himself to us and renew us from the inside out. If Jesus rose from the dead, it means we are not just atoms or accidents; we are known completely and loved immensely, and we are being invited to live a life of deep purpose and meaning that nothing can ever take away.

If Jesus rose from the dead. But that's a huge *if*, isn't it? You might be feeling pretty sceptical. You might think: *maybe* there's a God or life beyond death, but surely there's no way for us to really know!

I can sympathise with that; I'm naturally very sceptical myself. I've been wrestling with questions and doubts around this for years—and I want to show you the things that have convinced me that the resurrection of Jesus really happened. I think we can believe it, not by blind faith or childish optimism but by being rationally convinced. The resurrection of Jesus makes sense of the facts of history in a way no other explanation can, and it also makes sense of the whole universe.

So in the pages that follow, I'm hoping to do two big things:

- I want to show you that you actually can believe in the resurrection of Jesus and everything it means. It's credible and real.
- And I want to show you that it is spectacularly good news. The implications are profound, beautiful and exciting. If it's true, it's both life-affirming and life-transforming.

I don't know what you believe at the moment about life, death, morality or meaning, and I don't know what doubts and questions you have about those beliefs. But wherever we're coming from, we are all searching for answers that are both good and true. I think we can find them.

CHAPTER 1

HOPE, AND WHY IT MATTERS

"Hope is a powerful weapon."

Nelson Mandela wrote those words to his wife from a hard-labour prison on Robben Island where he had been locked up for seven years.[1] He would be in there for 20 more. Two more decades of back-breaking work in the quarry and lonely hours staring at prison walls. But somehow, Mandela held onto hope. When he was finally released, he hadn't hardened into vengefulness or crumbled into despair. He emerged with the strength of character to lead his country peacefully through the transformation he had longed for; and he was renowned all over the world for his *smile*. Hope turned out to be a very powerful weapon indeed.

If I'm honest, I used to be bored by talk about hope beyond death. It all sounded like "pie in the sky when you die" that made no real difference to me. But I realise now that I was missing something crucial. Genuine hope changes things in the present. A difficult journey feels totally different if we know where we're going. The same story could be either a heartbreaking tragedy or a beautiful epic, depending on how it ends. What we believe about tomorrow changes how we feel about today; it changes how we make sense of things and how we choose to live. Hope is powerful.

So before we dive into the rational question about whether Jesus really rose, we're going to think about why that question matters right now. This is relevant to all of us—whether we're feeling our frailty or we're young, fit and healthy—because life confronts us with urgent questions that we just can't answer if we have no idea what comes after death.

We're going to consider two of those questions: a personal question we face when we lose someone close to us, and a global question that rears its head whenever we watch the news. One is about love, the other about justice; but they both bring us back to the question of hope.

Love Versus Death

My grandad was the first person I ever sat with on their deathbed. As my brother and I held his hands, I wished that we could somehow hold on tight enough that we wouldn't have to let him go. But at the same time, the question pounding in my head was: let him go *where*? I think most of us who've lost someone will have had moments—maybe as we wait for the end to come, or after the funeral, or at a family wedding that they would have loved to see—where we find ourselves asking these kinds of questions. Have they really gone? Where are they now? Are "they" anywhere at all, or is there no "them" left?

We might talk about people "watching over us" or being "in a better place", but we don't know if we actually mean it, and we're scared to think about it too hard.

A couple of years ago, I attended the most moving funeral I've ever been to. It was for Marcel, a friend of my wife's. For all the years we'd known him, Marcel was a walking, talking explosion of joy. He had become a Christian when he was 18, and it had totally transformed him: he was one of the warmest people I'd ever met, utterly transparent, with a booming laugh that was wonderfully infectious. He was an actor; at the funeral we heard stories about him drawing an entire cast into animated discussions about God just before curtain-up at the National Theatre. We watched clips of him dancing exuberantly dressed as a caterpillar, for reasons I don't fully understand! But Marcel had died of an unusual heart condition in his thirties, leaving behind his wife and two young children. They were lost without him. It was unbearably sad.

No one dared offer hollow words of comfort that day. But there was a moment in the service that I will never forget, when they played a video that Marcel had recorded with a Christian theatre company. He was acting as John, one of Jesus' friends, in a scene retelling how John met Jesus after he'd risen from the dead. As Marcel spoke out John's description of Jesus—alive and real and right there with him in the room—it was obvious that the tears of joy and love welling up in the corners of his eyes weren't just a performance. At one point he looked into the camera and repeated the words of Jesus:

> I am the resurrection and the life. The one who believes in me will live, even though they die.[2]

You could see on Marcel's face that he really believed it. It was like he was preaching at his own funeral.

As I watched, it came home to me that Marcel was not gone for ever. If Jesus really had come back from the dead, then he could keep that promise: he could really give Marcel life beyond death. It came home to me that Marcel still existed, he still loved his wife and his kids, he still loved Jesus, and he was enjoying being alive with him at that very moment. So, in amongst the tears of grief and shock and confusion, there were also tears of poignant, certain joy. Tears of hope.

Some people teach us to be stoical about death. They say it's wise not to let ourselves get too attached to anything or anyone. Love is a strange glitch in the vast, impersonal machine of the universe, and that glitch will vanish in the end; we shouldn't try to fight that or hope for something more.[3] We can only find peace by surrendering to the inevitable.

But as I held my grandad's hand, love didn't feel like a glitch, and I didn't want to surrender. And if Jesus did rise from the dead, we don't *need* to surrender. The Easter story says that Jesus sacrificed his life in the ultimate act of love: his death was *for* us. If Jesus defeated death and rose to unstoppable life, then that means love is *stronger* than death, not weaker. Jesus' love for us is so strong that, if we believe in him, he will take hold of us and never let go. We will enjoy life with him for ever. It is death that will disappear one day, not love.

We might go months or years without considering what we think about this stuff. But my guess is that for all of us moments will come when we find that this matters immensely—that we need to know here and now what's really going to happen next.

But it's not just love that makes us ask that question. It also jumps out at us when we see the injustice in our world.

Will Justice Ever Come?

A friend of mine told me once that a charity he was involved with in Uganda was supporting the education of a ten-year-old girl. A local businessman had wanted to buy the house that this girl lived in, but her mother didn't want to sell. So this businessman raped the little girl. He then bribed the local police chief, so that when the girl's brother went to report the crime, they arrested *him* instead for no reason. My friend's charity worked hard to gather evidence against the businessman, but he was not convicted. He was never even charged with an offence. And he continues to run a successful business to this day.

I don't know how you feel reading something like that; I still feel my stomach churning with anger when I think about it. But the fact is, there's nothing unusual about that story. Whether it's through corruption, intimidation, or sheer force of arms, there are people all over this planet—in both poorer nations and rich ones—who've committed terrible evil without ever being called to account. And even if we manage in our generation to forge a better world, we are already too late for the countless murderers and warmongers who have lived out their days on earth without ever being brought to justice.

The problem is that if death is the end, then that's it. If death is the ultimate full stop, then that man's wealth will probably shield him for ever, and that girl will never get to see that what he did to her *matters*. If this world of politics and power is all there is, then as long as someone has enough power, there's no hope for justice at all.

But if Jesus rose from the dead, that's not true.

Paul of Tarsus was a man who claimed to have met Jesus soon after he'd been resurrected. He gave a speech about it in Athens a few years later, which ended like this:

> Now [God] commands all people everywhere to repent. For he has set a day when he will judge the world with justice by the man he has appointed. He has given proof of this to everyone by raising him from the dead.[4]

Jesus said that one day he will be the just judge of everyone who has ever lived.[5] According to Paul, if Jesus rose from the dead, that's emphatic proof that his claim was true. Earthly justice, with all its failings, is not the only justice there is; there's something better on its way.

Imagine the difference this makes for that Ugandan family. Death is not the end. There will be justice. More than that, the ultimate judge isn't some distant, uncaring deity—it's Jesus. This judge is compassionate. In fact, he cares so deeply about victims that he willingly became one. He was humiliated, brutalised and even killed; he plumbed the depths of human suffering and injustice.[6] So when Jesus judges the world, he will show exactly the right amount of compassion towards that little girl, and exactly the right amount of anger towards that businessman. His justice will show them both how much that little girl is truly worth. Whatever lies the world might have told her, on that day she will know that she matters.[7]

Martin Luther King Jr. once said this:

> Evil may so shape events that Caesar will occupy a palace and Christ a cross, but one day that same Christ will rise up and split history into A.D. and B.C., so that even the life of Caesar must be dated by his name.[8]

It may seem as if political power and brute force rule the world, but ultimately Jesus will have the final word. If Jesus rose, then justice will triumph. If Jesus is in charge of the eternal future, no one will be forgotten and nothing will be swept under the carpet: *every* wrong will be put right.

This is a bit of a double-edged sword for people like me and you. We have all been wronged, and we want justice to declare that what was done to us matters. But we have all also wronged other people, and they matter too. For many of us, if we take an honest look back at our lives, we realise that perfect justice is something we both long for and dread.

Yet Jesus' death and resurrection are not just a promise of judgment but also an offer of forgiveness and redemption—as we'll see later. This means his hope is "a powerful weapon", but it's not a weapon meant to be brandished against others, to crush people with guilt. Jesus' kind of hope humbles the proud and comforts the conscience-stricken. It gives courage to the weary and strengthens the weak. It's powerful not to harm, but to heal.

But there's one vital qualification to make.

"Hope Is a Dangerous Thing"

It's become quite intellectually fashionable in recent years for people to say, "I live my life *as if* God is real" or "*as if* Jesus rose". This might mean they have moral values that they can't explain from an atheist perspective. Or they might take the resurrection as a metaphor: there's always light at the end of the tunnel, winter gives way to spring, and "life" can come out of "death" in even the bleakest circumstances. The resurrection as a symbol of hope sounds lovely and inspiring; but the problem is, if it's *only* a symbol, then that hope is false and misleading.

In the 1994 film *The Shawshank Redemption*, prison inmate Andy confidently tells a veteran prisoner, Red, that hope is something the guards can never take away from you. But Red replies, "Hope? Let me tell you something, my friend: hope is a dangerous thing. Hope can drive a man insane." He's got a point. If you're in prison and there is genuinely no way out, you're far better off facing the facts and getting used to it than fixating on an inspirational fantasy. Hope that isn't rooted in something real is ultimately cruel, because it will let us down when we need it most. When we lose someone we love, a vague metaphorical hope will be no comfort at all.

But the first followers of Jesus insisted that they weren't writing a metaphor or a myth. One of them wrote, "If Christ has not been raised, our preaching is useless and so is your faith. More than that, we are then found to be false witnesses about God, for we have testified about God that he raised Christ from the dead."[9] In other words, this is either real or it's a pointless and immoral lie. My sceptical brain resonates with this massively. We're not meant to just ask ourselves, "Do these ideas sound nice to me?" We're meant to investigate honestly whether they are true.

That's why the *if* in this book is so important. If Jesus is dead and buried somewhere, Christianity is a dangerous delusion. But if Jesus is actually alive, he's so much more than a motivational story. If Jesus rose, we know that death is only temporary, love will last for ever, and every wrong will be put right. And that's just the start! It would mean that there's a living, loving God, and you and I matter to him. It would mean that he's inviting us right now to join his family and play a vital part in what he's doing to redeem this world.

So the question is: is it true? And how could we possibly know?

FOR REFLECTION OR CONVERSATION

- *What do you think about life after death?*
- *What has led you to those ideas?*

CHAPTER 2

LIFE, THE UNIVERSE AND EVERYTHING

How do you know that you're reading a book right now? How do you know you're not being tricked into believing that by a mad scientist who's got your brain in a vat? If the scientist was doing his or her job properly, there would be no experiment you could run to prove it either way. This is a classic philosophy question, designed to show that we can't 100% prove almost anything we think we know.

But of course, for all intents and purposes, you *do* know that you're a human with a body who's reading a book, and not just a brain bubbling away in a jar. You know that because, as *The Oxford Companion to Philosophy* helpfully puts it, "The conclusion that you really are looking at a book … explains the aggregate of your experiences better than the mad scientist hypothesis or any other competing view."[10] You can trust that the book is real, your hands are real and your eyes are real, because that explanation makes much better sense of the facts than any other. It resolves all the evidence you have in a simple and elegant way.

In other words, the way we know anything at all is the same way a detective in a murder mystery knows who did it: we find the explanation that makes the best sense of all the evidence.[11]

In some of the most brilliantly written mysteries, that whole explanation hinges on one specific fact. Before the detective discovers that crucial piece of evidence, the case seems completely unsolvable; but once she has it, everything else suddenly falls into place. Once we've seen that one, vital thing, the whole mystery makes sense.

When it comes to the great mystery of life, the resurrection of Jesus is that pivotal piece of evidence. We might be tempted to think of the resurrection as a freak one-off event that sticks out like a sore thumb from everything else we know; it seems like a weird anomaly we don't really understand but can probably ignore. But actually, it's the opposite.

Our existence is a huge mystery stuffed full of smaller mysteries: every time we think we've worked something out, it reveals an even stranger puzzle underneath. We all want to find meaningful answers to the deep questions of life, but it can sometimes feel totally overwhelming because as soon as we start looking, we're deluged with a thousand different ideas, philosophies and beliefs. How on earth are we meant to make sense of it all? Where would we even start?

But the resurrection of Jesus is actually the perfect place to start, because if it's real, it's a kind of skeleton key with the potential to unlock many different mysteries. It's a concrete historical event we can genuinely investigate and get to grips with, but it also offers us an elegant and beautiful explanation for who we are and why we're here. The resurrection is the one thing that could actually make sense of everything else.

How Do We Explain This Universe?

Let's start with the most basic mystery of all. I grew up with the impression that science had already answered most of the important questions about our existence and would soon polish off the rest—but it turns out that's not true. Science has deepened our understanding in beautiful and world-changing ways, but it just can't answer some of the most obvious and important questions we have. Most fundamentally of all: why is the universe here?

Stephen Hawking explains in the conclusion of *A Brief History of Time* that this is a mystery which science by its nature could never solve:

> Even if there is [a complete scientific theory of everything], it is just a set of rules and equations. What is it that breathes fire into the equations and makes a universe for them to describe? The usual approach of science of constructing a mathematical model cannot answer the questions of why there should be a universe for the model to describe. Why does the universe go to all the bother of existing?[12]

To clarify, this isn't a matter of dreamy, philosophical people searching for a deeper purpose behind why they exist. It's about seeking a reasonable explanation for the existence of anything at all. The problem is that everything in the material universe—all scientifically observable *stuff*—is caused by something before it. If you were watching a pool table with a ball sitting still on it, and the ball suddenly started rolling across the table, you wouldn't think, "Oh, of course—that makes sense." You'd think, "What made it do that? What moved it?" Because you know that everything that happens in the material world is *caused* by something.

Science has done a fascinating job of tracing that chain of cause and effect back as far as it can go: to the Big Bang. The Big Bang is extremely difficult for normal people like me to imagine, because it wasn't just an explosion at a point in space way back in time: physicists say it was the bursting into being of all the matter in the universe, and space itself, and time itself.[13] So if we try to explain scientifically what *caused* the Big Bang, we get very stuck indeed. We have no scientific evidence that there was anything before it—or indeed any time or space for anything "before" it to be in!

Several theories have been suggested. Perhaps we're in an oscillating universe, and the Big Bang was caused by the "Big Crunch" of a universe that existed before this one. Or perhaps there's an expanding multiverse, and universes continually pop into being within it. But the problem is that if we offer a purely physical theory for what caused the start of our universe, we've just pushed the same problem back a step. As Ian Hutchinson, Professor of Nuclear Science at MIT, puts it: "If there is ... a multiverse ... then one should instead ask what caused the multiverse to exist? ... Claims that cosmology has solved the problem of first cause ... are philosophical nonsense."[14]

The philosophy professor and co-founder of Wikipedia Larry Sanger explains it like this:

> Science says the Big Bang was the beginning of the universe. But whatever had a beginning has to have had an explanation. As this is the beginning of matter itself, it cannot have a material cause; thus *it must have an immaterial cause* (whatever that might be like).[15]

In other words, for the material world to have got going in the first place, there must have been something to start it that isn't part of the material world and doesn't play by the same rules. There must be something that is real, but isn't a physical thing. Something *super*natural.

I'm not offering this as an inescapable proof that God exists—I'm saying it's a mystery we all need to ponder. The existence of the universe itself is a pretty huge piece of evidence, so we should be keeping our eyes open for an explanation that could make sense of it.

And it's not just the universe existing. Life coming about within the universe is another mystery all by itself. Francis Crick, one of the scientists who helped discover DNA, considered the origin of life on earth to be "almost a miracle".[16] What makes it such a mystery is that DNA is information. Words are information made up of letters; computer code is information made up of noughts and ones; and DNA is information made up of proteins. At a fundamental level, they all work in the same way. But words and code are written by people. Information doesn't emerge randomly: it only comes from minds. So, how could DNA have come into existence unless there was a mind of some sort to generate it? Crick's attempt to account for this was to suggest that our planet might have been seeded with simple life forms by advanced extraterrestrials![17] Again we need to ask, what's the best explanation?

And then there's everything else. How do we explain consciousness? Where does beauty come from? How does music convey meaning? How can it be that maths corresponds to the real world? It turns out that our whole existence is a tangled bundle of mysteries that can't satisfactorily be solved unless there's something non-material behind the material world—some kind of god.

But how are we supposed to *know* if there is a supernatural being of some sort behind the universe? And if it did exist, how could we possibly know what it was? Or *who* it was? Our only hope would be if the supernatural being introduced itself somehow. Logically we have to ask, is there anything in human history that plausibly could have been the Creator introducing itself to us?

And that leads us to a more zoomed-in mystery—one that I think anyone who wants to have intellectual integrity needs to get to grips with as well.

How Do We Explain Jesus?

Who on earth was Jesus? It's a surprisingly difficult question. Most people believe that Jesus was a "great teacher", or "a prophet or spiritual leader, but not God".[18] And all the evidence certainly does suggest that he was a brilliant moral teacher who lived a compellingly good life. Yet as we read the accounts of Jesus' life, we find that, in amongst the moral teachings that are so wise and beautiful that they've transformed our world, there are also a lot of shocking statements. Jesus claims that he personally can forgive people's sins.[19] He says he is going to judge the world at the end of time.[20] He says he's always existed.[21] At one point one of his followers says to him, "Show us the Father"—asking if they can somehow know God directly. Jesus replies, "Don't you know me, Philip, even after I have been among you such a long time? Anyone who has seen me has seen the Father."[22] In other words, *If you've seen me, you have seen God.*

All that creates quite a conundrum. Those claims are either true or they're not. If they're not, and Jesus was just a human like me and you, but *he made all those claims about himself anyway*, then he wasn't a very good moral teacher or spiritual guru after all. He was either wildly delusional or lying on purpose to lure people into a cult. With Jesus there are really only three options: he was a lunatic, a liar, or he was the Lord of the universe. As the author C.S. Lewis put it:

> You can shut Him up for a fool, you can spit at Him and kill Him as a demon; or you can fall at His feet and call Him Lord and God. But let us not come with any patronising nonsense about His being a great human teacher. He has not left that open to us. He did not intend to.[23]

This makes Jesus a unique figure in history. No one else has ever started a significant religion or movement while claiming not just to be a messenger or teacher but to actually be *God* revealing himself. In an overwhelming world of different philosophies and religious ideas, this uniqueness is very practically helpful. It means that instead of drowning amongst a thousand competing claims about the way to God as we try and fail to weigh them all against each other, we can focus our thinking on a fixed point. Jesus claimed to be something very different, and we can start by trying to find out if he was telling the truth.

This is where the resurrection becomes so crucial. If Jesus rose from the dead, that would be very significant evidence that he was telling the truth. On the other hand, we saw in the last chapter that the first followers of Jesus said that if he didn't rise from the dead, the whole thing is a pointless lie. If it didn't happen, we can discard Christianity entirely and move on.

The resurrection turns out to be the perfect place to start if we want to make sense of life. It's the bit of evidence we most need to examine, because if it really happened, it's the pivotal piece of the puzzle that allows all the others to fall into place. It would show us who Jesus was, and in the process provide a coherent explanation for our universe. It would vindicate Jesus' claim to be the Creator stepping into human history to introduce himself.

So, then, we need to look at the evidence.

FOR REFLECTION OR CONVERSATION

- *If Jesus was really God, what difference do you think that would make?*

CHAPTER 3

THE EVIDENCE

"Faith is not a leap in the dark. It's a commitment based on evidence."

I find those words from Professor John Lennox extremely helpful, because I grew up hearing lots of talk (both outside and inside the church) about taking a "leap of faith". It's easy to get the impression that when Christianity asks us to have "faith" in Jesus, it's doing something like Peter Pan in the old pantomime: if we all shout, "I do believe in fairies! I do! I do!" loud enough, then Tinkerbell will come back to life. But that's not right at all. The kind of faith Christianity asks for is grounded trust. It's not shutting our eyes and making a wild leap into the unknown; it's more like marrying someone you've come to trust for all sorts of solid reasons.

So when it comes to the resurrection, we shouldn't be asking, "Can I summon up the 'faith' from inside myself to believe this?" It's a historical event. We should be looking at the historical data and asking, "What makes the most sense?" Which explanation requires the least blind faith? We should work this out the same way we've worked out everything else we know: what makes the best sense of all the evidence?

The simplest way to examine the evidence is to lay out five key facts, and then the five main explanations for those things that have been offered by historians.

The Big Three Facts

We'll start with the big three. These are the central historical facts of the case which serious historians generally agree on—atheist, agnostic, Jewish and Christian historians alike. The overwhelming consensus is that we know these things happened. What people disagree on is how we should explain them.

1. Jesus died by crucifixion.

Jesus was a historical person who lived 2,000 years ago in a part of the Middle East that had relatively recently become an occupied territory of the Roman Empire. In around AD 30 he was executed by the authority of the governor, Pontius Pilate. This is, in the words of the sceptical scholar John Dominic Crossan, a fact "as sure as anything historical can ever be."[24] We even have non-Christian sources, writing within a lifetime of the events, who tell us that Jesus was crucified.[25]

2. His disciples were convinced they had met him alive again.

Historians agree that Jesus' followers *claimed* to have seen him back from the dead. But they also agree that these men and women must have been *genuinely convinced* that they had seen him.

Why? Because if they weren't convinced, there is simply no way they would have done what they did. We have historical accounts of other Jewish figures in the first and second centuries who, like Jesus, claimed to be the Messiah—the liberating king whom God had promised to give to the Jewish people. Each of these figures gathered a following to fight for freedom from Rome. But when those would-be Messiahs were defeated and killed, their movements disbanded completely; or in some situations a group chose someone else, perhaps a relative, and transferred their hopes onto the new leader.[26] Either way, death was felt to be definitive proof that these Messiah-like figures were not actually the real deal.

But not with Jesus. Instead of going into hiding or choosing a new leader, the disciples of Jesus started announcing that he had risen from the dead. They claimed that they had seen him themselves, and that his resurrection proved that he really was the Messiah. They accused Jewish leaders of having conspired to kill their own promised king, and proclaimed that *Jesus* was the true Lord of the world, not the Roman emperor.

This was unsurprisingly not popular with either the Jewish or the Roman authorities, who attempted to brutally silence the disciples. There is abundant evidence for this from both Christian and non-Christian sources close to the events.[27] Many of Jesus' followers were arrested and tortured; some, perhaps most, were eventually killed. But there is no record of any one of them going back on their insistence that Jesus was alive.

The thing is that no one would risk their life for something they *knew* wasn't true. And the disciples weren't just willing to die for a belief they'd picked up second-hand—something they'd been told by other people and become convinced of. They were claiming that Jesus was alive and that they had witnessed him themselves. This is why even an atheist scholar like Gerd Lüdemann says:

> It may be taken as *historically certain* that Peter and the disciples had experiences after Jesus' death in which Jesus appeared to them as the risen Christ.[28]

Lüdemann thinks these experiences were hallucinations, which we'll discuss later—but for now, what's clear is that something definitely happened which convinced the disciples that they'd met Jesus back from the dead. If they hadn't been sure of this, why on earth would they have kept insisting on it, even under the threat of death?

3. Opponents of Christianity were also convinced that they had met Jesus alive again.

This one sounds like the most unbelievable of the big three facts. Surely only people who were already followers of Jesus would claim that they'd seen him alive after he'd risen from the dead? But we know this is true because we literally have it first-hand. We have many letters written by a man called Paul of Tarsus in the 40s and 50s AD. He was a zealous member of the Pharisees—the Jewish group most opposed to Jesus—and he was actively persecuting the first Christians as heretics. Then he had an experience which he described as the resurrected Jesus appearing to him.[29] This encounter changed the course of Paul's life and led him to become a key advocate of the Jesus movement—gladly suffering the consequences. Many of his letters are written from prison, and we have multiple sources telling us that he was eventually executed for spreading this subversive message.[30]

There is also a strong consensus that James, the half-brother of Jesus, was sceptical about his claims before his death but was converted by seeing him back from the dead, and became a widely known leader in the early church.[31]

So we know that it wasn't just people who had followed Jesus to begin with. At least two opponents of Christianity thought they saw him back from the dead and changed their minds because of it.

Two More Helpful Bits of Historical Data

Along with the Big Three facts, there are two more things that are helpful to know as we try to find an explanation.

4. The witnesses said that Jesus' tomb was empty.

We have a number of reports from witnesses who claim to have seen Jesus alive. Each of them involves a statement that his tomb was empty—only the graveclothes were left behind. That's significant because it tells us that when the disciples started saying that Jesus had risen, they didn't mean that his spirit lived on in some abstract or ghostly sense. They meant that his body had returned to life in such a way that they couldn't find it in the tomb anymore.

5. The Christian movement exploded immediately.
It's also good to know that the message about the risen Jesus spread remarkably widely and quickly. Jesus died in AD 30 or 33, and we have letters which can be dated to the 40s and 50s, written by Christians to groups of believers spread out across the regions that we know today as Greece, Italy and Turkey.[32] We even have the Roman historian Tacitus telling us that by AD 64 there was a "vast multitude" of Christians in Rome.[33] Rome is as far from Jerusalem as Edinburgh is from Morocco—further than Canada is from Mexico! The resurrection message had spread far and wide, very fast indeed.

So What's the Best Explanation?

In 2,000 years of people wrestling with these basic facts, there have only really been a few alternative explanations suggested. Let's think through the options.

Theory 1: Jesus didn't really die.

This is often called "swoon theory". The idea is that Jesus just fainted on the cross, and then revived at some point in the tomb. The main problem with this is that Jesus was executed by the Romans—and if the Romans were experts in anything, it was killing people.

There is no historical record of anyone surviving a crucifixion; the soldiers knew when someone was dead, and they knew how to make sure of it. On top of that, one of the reports accidentally includes a detail—that when a soldier stuck a spear into Jesus' side to check he was dead, what looked like blood and water flowed out—which turns out 2,000 years later to be medical proof of death.[34]

But even if we ignored all of that, this theory would still be totally implausible. The idea that a Jesus who was barely clinging onto life after a brutal Roman flogging and crucifixion could have convinced the disciples that he had triumphed over death and was going to live for ever is ridiculous. If he had somehow managed to get out of his tomb and stagger over the threshold to meet them, they would have tried to tend his wounds, not worship him![35]

Theory 2: The disciples moved the body and made it all up.

This theory isn't popular with historians because it completely contradicts what we know about the witnesses (facts 2 and 3 above). If the disciples had perpetrated some kind of hoax by moving the body, they would obviously have known it wasn't true—but there are many good reasons why historians across the religious spectrum agree that the disciples were convinced they had met the risen Jesus. Even Bart Ehrman, a sceptical agnostic scholar, is confident that they thought they were telling the truth; he just thinks they were deluded.[36]

The central reason why historians agree on this is that there was simply no motive for the disciples to come up with a lie like that. It wasn't a political grab for power, and it certainly wasn't for their own personal gain—rather, it put them in huge danger.[37] Whatever people believe about what actually happened, no serious historians think it was all an elaborate hoax.

The other thing you'll discover if you read any of the four Gospels (the biographies of Jesus by Mark, Matthew, Luke and John) is that they all say that the first witnesses to the empty tomb and the risen Jesus were *women*. That might not seem like a big deal to us, but at the time it was a real shock. At that point in both Roman and Jewish society, women were looked down on and considered less rational than men. A woman's testimony wasn't considered valid in a Jewish law court.[38] I love that in the middle of that culture, Jesus still chose to make women the first eyewitnesses! But this doesn't just show us that Jesus trusts and values women; it's also compelling evidence that these stories weren't made up. If you wanted to tell a story to convince people that Jesus had risen, there's no way you would have presented as your first witness someone who would soon be mocked as a "hysterical female".[39] The accounts we have are the kinds of stories that would only have been told *if that was what actually happened.*[40]

And besides all that, the hoax theory completely fails to explain why Paul, who wasn't a disciple at all, was also convinced he'd met Jesus. It simply doesn't cover the facts of the case.

Theory 3: The appearances were hallucinations. This is the main argument that atheist historians have turned to over the years, but it has been dealt some major blows by modern scientific enquiry. The two appearances of the risen Jesus for which we have the strongest evidence are his appearance to the eleven disciples, and his appearance to Paul. Based on what studies have shown, it is vanishingly unlikely that either of these appearances could have been hallucinations.

Some historians have suggested that the grief felt by Jesus' followers might have generated hallucinations. This kind of thing can happen, particularly amongst elderly people who've lost spouses after decades living together. But consider Paul—the man who started off persecuting Christians but then became convinced Jesus was alive. Paul hadn't spent any time with Jesus, and he wasn't grieving his death. There's no plausible psychological explanation for Paul hallucinating Jesus at all.

Jesus seeming to appear to the eleven disciples is even harder to explain, because we know that a group of people all having the same hallucination at the same time simply doesn't happen. The nature of hallucinations is that they happen inside your head, much like a dream, so they can't be shared. Gary Sibcy, a licensed clinical psychologist with a PhD in the subject, writes:

> I have surveyed the professional literature (peer-reviewed journal articles and books) written by psychologists, psychiatrists, and other relevant healthcare professionals during the past two decades and have yet to find a single

> documented case of a group hallucination, that is, an event for which more than one person purportedly shared in a visual or other sensory perception where there was clearly no external referent.[41]

For hallucinations to explain even just these two key appearances, it would require a combination of incredibly unlikely things to have happened. It would be like rolling a pair of dice that each have hundreds of sides, and getting a double six—and then rolling them eleven more times (for the eleven disciples) and getting eleven more double sixes. And even then it would completely fail to explain the rest of the evidence, such as the witnesses' insistence that the tomb was empty. Hallucinations alone would never have convinced anyone that Jesus was physically alive again in his body—they would have assumed they were seeing his spirit or his ghost. Even a one-in-a-million fluke of crazy psychological coincidences wouldn't have led the earliest Christians to believe what we know they actually believed.

Theory 4: It's just a myth that emerged over time. People often claim that there's a historical core of stuff about Jesus that did really happen, but then suggest that the supernatural bits like the resurrection are legends that were gradually added over time.

The big problem with this idea is that the claim of Jesus' resurrection didn't emerge over time. As I've already mentioned, we have letters of Paul which scholars date to the 40s or 50s AD; in these letters, Paul not only clearly believes that Jesus rose from the dead but also assumes that *all the Christians he's writing to* know that as well.[42] So the resurrection was a universal belief in the Christian community within 20 years of it happening. That's well within the lifetime of the eyewitnesses, and leaves nowhere near enough time for a myth to develop through a "telephone game" process of gradual exaggeration.

Even more striking, Paul quotes a "creedal formula"—a kind of easy-to-memorise summary statement—about Jesus dying, rising and appearing to lots of named witnesses, which he says he "received" from other believers. This happened most likely when he met with the original disciples in Jerusalem—a meeting historians date within the 30s AD. That's seriously early.

There is not a scrap of evidence for any "original" version of Christianity that didn't believe in the resurrection—just solid evidence that it was at the very heart of Christianity right from the start. Even later on, in the 100s and 200s AD, when there were all kinds of major doctrinal disagreements in the church, none of them were about whether Jesus rose from the dead.

But it's not just the dates that make the myth theory implausible. If you stop to think about motivations for a moment, the idea of Christians adding the resurrection to the account of Jesus' life makes no sense. As we've seen, even the most sceptical scholars think that the early Christians honestly believed what they preached and wrote, and had no intention to mislead people. Some argue that they could have added extra bits out of a pious eagerness to make Jesus look even better, or to offer more support for things they already believed about him. But these were devoutly religious people, and both the Jewish tradition they came from and the Lord they followed were emphatic in condemning lying and commending truthfulness.[43] How could these early Christians possibly have dared to *invent* something as significant as Jesus' resurrection?

And why would they have wanted to? Any individual or community who is supposed to have made these "embellishments" must have believed in Jesus already, based on a version of the story without the resurrection. If it was enough for them, why would they have thought it needed improving?

On top of that, the scholar N.T. Wright has demonstrated in his 800-page book *The Resurrection of the Son of God* that if the early Christians did imagine or invent stories about Jesus coming back to life after death, there is simply no way they would have come up with the kind of resurrection we see described in the Gospels. They would either have imagined a purely spiritual, ghost-like existence based on Greek and Roman ideas of the immortal soul, or they would have drawn on texts in the Hebrew Bible (what Christians call the Old Testament) to imagine a resuscitated body restored to normality. What they actually describe is a resurrected Jesus who is definitely physical and not just ghostly—he eats fish and touches people—but who is also definitely different to normal, able to appear and disappear at will and to walk through locked doors.[44]

In other words, not only was there no opportunity and no motivation for the resurrection to be added to the Christian message over time, the accounts we have of it are simply *too weird* to be myths.

A Leap of Faith?

When we examine these four explanations, even quite briefly, it becomes clear that all of them are very difficult to accept rationally. To believe any of them requires us to close our eyes to known historical facts and take a leap of blind faith.

Several years ago, the Christian Union at Bristol University put on an event called The Great Resurrection Debate. They put a big advert in the student newspaper, and offered a cash prize of £500 for the person who gave the best explanation for the evidence I've just outlined, other than Jesus actually rising from the dead. They put together a panel of legal professionals who weren't Christians to sift through the entries, chaired by a judge. At the debate itself, the three best entries had ten minutes to present their explanation. The winner was a version of the swoon theory. But two intriguing things happened: the judge—who was not a Christian—said in his closing remarks that none of the theories he'd heard would stand up in a court of law; and the winner said in his acceptance speech that he didn't believe his own theory. Later that year, he became a Christian.

The thing is, if none of the alternatives stand up to scrutiny, there's only one explanation left.

Theory 5: Jesus actually rose from the dead.
This would make sense of all the historical facts. It explains the appearances to the disciples, and to Paul and James; it explains the reports of the empty tomb; it explains why the witnesses were willing to risk suffering and death rather than deny what they'd seen; and it explains how anyone ever came to believe that a man crucified as a criminal was actually the God and Saviour of the world. It makes far better sense of the facts we have than any other theory. It fits.

So while some people say that Christianity requires you to stop thinking rationally and just believe blindly, that's not the case at all. In fact, history seems to suggest that by far the safest option if you don't want to believe in Jesus is to refuse to think rationally about this.

In the early 1920s, a lawyer and journalist called Frank Morison set out to write a book explaining how the false myth of the resurrection had come about. As he did his research, he became convinced it was actually true, and ultimately wrote his book the other way around, as an argument for the truth of the resurrection—it's called *Who Moved the Stone?* In 1981, Lee Strobel, the legal editor of the *Chicago Tribune*, decided to investigate the evidence because his wife had become a Christian and he wanted to show her that she was being misled. In the process, he became convinced that it was *him* who had been misled and wrote a book called *The Case for Christ*. In 1996, J. Warner Wallace, a decorated murder detective, began to apply the approach he used to solve cold cases to the question of Jesus. He became convinced, began to follow Jesus, and his book is called *Cold-Case Christianity*. In the 2000s, Nabeel Qureshi was a medical student and a devout Muslim, who loved his family and faith community and enjoyed debating with other religions. He developed a friendship with a Christian in which they challenged each other to objectively investigate the evidence for both faiths. After years of study and discussion, Nabeel became convinced—especially about the death and resurrection of Jesus—and sacrificed a huge amount to become a Christian. His book is called *Seeking Allah, Finding Jesus*.

So if you want to avoid becoming convinced of this stuff, it seems like it's very dangerous to think about it too deeply. Don't examine the evidence, don't engage with the arguments! You're safest just shrugging it off and thinking about something else.

Maybe a part of you wants to do exactly that. That's what a friend of mine told me when I showed her a draft of this chapter. She said she felt a resistance to the evidence, but admitted she wasn't sure where this resistance came from. She hadn't been convinced by an alternative theory or anything like that—there was just a big part of her that wanted to say, "I guess we don't know what happened" and stop thinking about it.

If you're feeling that resistance too, can I gently encourage you to push back at it a bit? If this is real, it makes sense of our lives and our world in a way that is seriously good news. As we'll begin to see in the rest of this book, if Jesus did rise from the dead, then we are living in a story that is far better and more beautiful than we ever expected. So it's absolutely worthwhile to push past our discomfort and wrestle with this honestly.

It's worth not just questioning the evidence, but questioning our doubts too.

FOR REFLECTION OR CONVERSATION

- *What do you think happened?*
- *Are there further questions you need answers to?*

CHAPTER 4

WHAT MAKES YOU HESITATE?

A while ago I stumbled across an interview with a comedian who had been asked about the afterlife. He said:

> Religious people might think [life] goes on after death. My feeling is that if that is the case it would be nice if just one person came back and let us know it was all fine, all confirmed. Of all the billions of people who have died, if just one of them could come through the clouds and say, you know, "It's me, Jeanine, it's brilliant, there's a really good spa", that would be great.[45]

The cheesy Christian response is obvious: "Aha! If just one person came back, that would be proof enough, would it? Well, *one* person has come back!" But I think the comedian's point is that he'd need to see Jeanine. He'd need to hear it from the horse's mouth. And we can't see Jesus, can we?

I think most of us instinctively feel like that. I know

I do. For something this important—a claim this weird and world-changing—surely we'd need to see it to believe it.

Doubting Thomas

But it's worth noticing that this isn't a new thing. It's not that modern people with the help of science have become wise and sceptical, whereas in the past if you said, "I heard Jesus rose from the dead," everyone was gullible enough to swallow it instantly. No: people have always known that on the whole, dead bodies stay where you left them. When you look at people's reactions in the Bible's accounts of the resurrection, some are sceptical, others are baffled, but no one just takes it in their stride! It turns out that this has *always* been hard to believe.

My favourite sceptic of the lot is Thomas. John, one of Jesus' closest friends, writes about how it was Mary Magdalene who first met the resurrected Jesus. Then later that day Jesus walked through a locked door and John himself saw him, along with a group of the other disciples. But Thomas, for whatever reason, missed it. John explains:

> Now Thomas (also known as Didymus), one of the Twelve, was not with the disciples when Jesus came. So the other disciples told him, "We have seen the Lord!"
>
> But he said to them, "Unless I see the nail marks in his hands and put my finger where the nails were, and put my hand into his side, I will not believe."[46]

All his friends insist they saw Jesus, but Thomas refuses to take their word for it. He says he can't believe it unless he can see Jesus for himself. In fact, he goes beyond "seeing is believing" and says that *touching* is believing! He won't believe a word they say until he can put his fingers in Jesus' nail-wounds, and his hand into the hole a centurion's spear had made in Jesus' abdomen. It's a gruesome image, but maybe Thomas is being gory on purpose to remind the others that Jesus was very dead. If he's going to believe that someone's alive again after that, he's going to need to see the proof first-hand. Literally.

Instinctively, I admire Thomas. At first glance he seems independent-minded, rational, almost scientific. But then when I think about it a bit more, I'm not so sure. Imagine if we tried to live by "seeing is believing" consistently. How much would I actually know if I refused to believe anything I couldn't see for myself?

History would be off the syllabus straight away. Most of geography would be tricky without an infinite travel budget, and even then I'd need a *lot* of patience to study coastal erosion, and a daredevil attitude for the volcanoes. In fact, if I stuck to "seeing is believing" I would even be useless at science. The only way scientific knowledge progresses is through people believing the findings of others' research. If I refused to believe anything I hadn't seen proof of myself, I'd need a couple of lifetimes in the lab just to get a GCSE. The truth is that to learn anything useful, we always have to believe the testimony of other people whom we accept as trustworthy.

So here's Thomas, with a whole group of his friends insisting they've seen Jesus. They've got no reason to lie to him, and they can't all be mistaken. What's the reasonable thing to do? On reflection, I think Thomas really should have followed the evidence. He should have believed the testimony of people he had reason to trust.

Paradigm Shift

So why did Thomas find that so hard to do? Probably for the same reason that it's hard for us to believe today: the resurrection just didn't fit with the idea of the world he had in his head.

Thomas Kuhn, the revered 20th-century philosopher of science, argued that new discoveries in science are always resisted at first. He explained that scientists always have an idea of how everything works—a "paradigm"—and naturally try to fit into it any new data they observe. To discover something that doesn't fit is an uncomfortable and discouraging experience. If the scientist can't get it to fit their paradigm, they must either ignore the new data or search for a new paradigm that makes sense of it. Kuhn showed that it is only through this difficult, uncomfortable process that science advances and our understanding of reality improves.[47]

It's the same for all of us who aren't scientists. We all have an idea in our heads of how the world works, of what's possible and what's not—a "worldview". When someone tells us something that fits neatly into that, it feels obvious and natural. But if we come across something that doesn't fit, we struggle to make sense of it. It feels implausible, like it can't be right. It's an uncomfortable experience. So we might dismiss this thing and try to forget about it. Or sometimes we start digging a little deeper and wondering if there could be a different understanding of the world which *would* be able to explain it. That process is confusing, disorientating and sometimes quite frightening. But Kuhn's point is, you can't get to truth without going through that discomfort. That's just what learning something important feels like.

Thomas's worldview—his paradigm—was that of a 1st-century Jew. He might have agreed with the school of Jewish thought which said there was no life after death at all, but it's more likely that he held the popular view that there would be a resurrection of all Jews at the end of history. Based on various promises in the Hebrew Scriptures, he would have believed that one day God would come down to earth, put a stop to the world as we know it, destroy evil, and bring his people back to life to live in a whole new age.[48] It was all going to happen at once, and it was going to be extremely obvious—you really couldn't miss it. If that's what Thomas believed, then the idea that *one* person had been raised from the dead in the middle of history while everyone else carried on as normal would have seemed totally bizarre. It didn't fit.

I grew up with a very different worldview to this, but the resurrection of Jesus didn't fit neatly with mine either. If you'd asked me what happens after we die, I might have said something vague about our souls being with God, but somehow the idea that Jesus rose from the dead in the flesh and in the middle of history felt a lot harder to swallow. I think that was because I felt that science had proven that miracles don't happen. So, let's examine that part of our worldview for a moment.

Science and Miracles

For anyone who's grown up in the same Western, science-driven culture as me, I suspect this is partly why the resurrection *feels* impossible to believe—regardless of all the historical evidence. We've all picked up the impression from somewhere (possibly Richard Dawkins) that miracles can't happen, and that we know that now thanks to science. Miracles can't happen, and therefore Jesus can't have risen from the dead.

But the more you examine this idea, the more it turns out to be a logical mistake. To say that miracles are "scientifically impossible" or that they "break the laws of nature" is to misunderstand both science and miracles.

The heart of the science we learn in school is the repeatable experiment, which establishes that if I do (A) under certain conditions, I can expect (B) to happen. That's a brilliant way to discover the regular workings of nature. But it can't tell you whether the way things *normally* work is the way they *always* work. (A) might lead to (B) under certain conditions, but at temperatures near absolute zero, or in the vacuum of space, something very different might happen. In other words, science is great at predicting what will happen, unless something unusual is going on that changes things. But the definition of a miracle is that something unusual *has* gone on that changed things: God has intervened.

I once heard Professor John Lennox explain it as follows. Imagine I put £50 in a drawer in my bedside table. Then the next night I put another £50 in. On the third night I open the drawer and find £0 in there. What would I think? "Oh no! The laws of mathematics have been broken!"? Probably not. I'd more likely think, "Oh no! The laws of England have been broken, and someone has stolen my money!" It would be ridiculous to say that the laws of mathematics prove that there is no such thing as theft. In the same way, it makes no sense to say that "the laws of nature" prove that there is no such thing as a miracle.

The question is, is the universe a locked drawer? If there is no God and the cosmos is just a closed system of physical stuff bouncing around, then of course, real miracles are impossible. But if there is a God, he can put his hand in the drawer and change things. In fact if God is the Creator, then the universe isn't just a drawer he can rummage in—it's a symphony he is personally conducting moment by moment. God may have created a natural world that usually operates in a regular rhythm, but he's still completely able to do something surprising whenever he chooses.

What all that adds up to is that science only "disproves miracles" if you assume to begin with that God doesn't exist! It's a circular argument: "There's no evidence that God exists; because the resurrection didn't happen; because miracles are impossible; because God doesn't exist." It doesn't work—it's like trying to pull yourself into the air by your shoelaces.

So if you grew up in a Western, Dawkins-influenced culture, you should probably be sceptical of your own instinctive scepticism. It's not rational to close our eyes to evidence that doesn't fit our preconceptions. It's not rational to say we'll only believe something if it can be proven in our favourite way—whether that's repeatable experiments or something completely different like mystical experiences. The truly rational approach is to be aware of our biases and assumptions, then pay attention to all the evidence and look for a paradigm that makes sense of the whole lot.

Looking Into the Camera

To be fair to Thomas, it can't have been easy to be the only one who hadn't seen Jesus. But after what must have been a very stressful week for him, he did finally get the chance to do what he'd been asking for.

> A week later his disciples were in the house again, and Thomas was with them. Though the doors were locked, Jesus came and stood among them and said, "Peace be with you!" Then he said to Thomas, "Put your finger here; see my hands. Reach out your hand and put it into my side. Stop doubting and believe."[49]

I love Jesus here. He's so gentle—he knows exactly what Thomas has been saying, and he's not angry with him. He's even humble enough to hold out his hands and offer Thomas the chance to touch the wounds. But it seems that once Jesus has made this offer, Thomas knows he doesn't need it:

> Thomas said to him, "My Lord and my God!"

Thomas realises straight away that the others were right, that Jesus is alive—and that this means he really is God in human form. Interestingly, Jesus doesn't tell Thomas to calm down and stop blaspheming; he accepts his worship. He essentially says, "It took you long enough!"

> Then Jesus told him, "Because you have seen me, you have believed; blessed are those who have not seen and yet have believed."

Jesus is saying, "Thomas, I'm so glad you've grasped the truth now, but you didn't really need this. You refused to believe what the others told you until after you'd seen me; but even more blessed than you will be the many people who believe that same testimony *before* they get to see me for themselves." It's a gentle challenge: Thomas thought he was being so reasonable, but he wasn't entitled to his own personal proof. He could have believed the testimony of the others. In fact, he *should* have believed them.

At which point John, who's writing the book, does that thing characters sometimes do in TV comedies where they turn away from the drama and look straight into the camera, right at the audience.

> Jesus performed many other signs in the presence of his disciples, which are not recorded in this book. But these are written that you may

> believe that Jesus is the Messiah, the Son of God, and that by believing you may have life in his name.

John looks out at whoever is reading his book, and he says, essentially, "We were telling Thomas the truth when we said that Jesus was alive, and he really should have believed it. And I've written these things down for you so that you can believe the truth too!"

We actually can believe this. It's hard to believe and it always has been. But that's precisely because it's so unique and so important. It demands that we change our paradigm and see the world differently, but the primary way we learn *anything* new is to believe the testimony of people we have reason to trust—and as we've seen, we have a lot of good reasons to trust what the disciples said about the resurrection.

John is saying to us, "We saw this with our own eyes, we know it's true, and we're willing to die for it. I've written it down so you can know it's true too. And let me tell you: if you believe in Jesus and embrace him for who he is, that won't just give you a different worldview: he will give you a whole new life."

A Modern-Day Thomas

Molly Worthen is a professional expert in religion. She earned a PhD in religious history from Yale before becoming a writer for the New York Times and a tenured professor of history at the University of North Carolina, Chapel Hill. She was one of the best-informed sceptics of Christianity out there. But then she got into an email conversation with the Christian author J.D. Greear while researching an article about his church. Greear challenged Worthen to look into the historical evidence for the resurrection, and what she found began to change her mind. As she applied her academic training to the subject, she began to be intellectually convinced.

In conversation with Rebecca McLaughlin on the *Confronting Christianity* podcast, she shared some of her thought process:

> I was thinking, you can't surely become a Christian simply by reading enough footnotes ... Surely there has to be some warm and fuzzy thing that happens internally! ... So I was praying for that, and I got nothing—it was just radio silence. But by the end of the summer, I found that, well, I'm not 99.9% persuaded that the resurrection happened, but I am definitely above 51%.[50]

It dawned on her that "the gap between me and Jesus is smaller than the gap behind me. So it's reasonable to jump." And by "jump" she means trusting and following Jesus: "Once you decide you believe a guy rose from the dead it starts to feel reasonable to say, 'Well, I will submit to him.'"

I think there's a lot of wisdom there. It's not wrong to ask God to show himself to us—that's a brilliant prayer for anyone to pray. In fact, why not pause at the end of this chapter and try it? But we don't need God to answer that prayer by writing a message in the clouds, giving us complete intellectual certainty, or allowing us to have a particular kind of emotional experience. God has already shown himself to us in the most personal and beautiful way possible. He has come to reveal himself in Jesus. And he has given us very good reasons to trust Jesus.

Worthen continues:

> Also I was persuaded by what a few Christians had said to me, which is: "Okay, Molly, you say you want this magical lovely feeling in your heart: it sounds like you're describing faith, the relationship [with God], and you can't expect to have that if you haven't entered the relationship." ... I still feel my faith is fragile—at some level I've got to talk myself into it every day—but then I talk to mature Christians who feel the same way! So I think I'm developing more of a healthy relationship with my doubt.

This is the kind of faith I think John is encouraging us to have. Not a brash certainty with no traces of doubt at all. Not discovering that we've started "feeling religious" all of a sudden. Just following the evidence until we realise that the gap between us and Jesus is smaller than the gap behind us, and deciding that we can trust him. As we begin trusting and following him, we will start to experience the reality of that new relationship.

But... what exactly is that reality? If we do walk through the door the resurrection opens for us, what do we discover on the other side? That's what I want to explore in the next chapter.

FOR REFLECTION OR CONVERSATION

- *Do you find the resurrected Jesus easy, hard or impossible to believe in?*
- *Why do you think that is?*

CHAPTER 5

REAL LIFE IN A NEW LIGHT

If Jesus did rise from the dead, it changes everything. Rewind with me to what it would have been like for Thomas when Jesus walked into the room. Your dead friend is standing there in front of you, alive. He looks you in the eye and says, "Peace be with you." You can see the nail wounds from the crucifixion in his outstretched hands.

It's like one of those moments in a great movie where something completely unexpected happens that sheds new light on everything that came before, opening up the possibility of a totally different ending. In an instant, Thomas's world has been turned upside down—or maybe the right way up.

The resurrection does that for us too. It's the plot twist at the heart of the true story of reality. It opens our eyes to see literally everything in a new light. So in this chapter I want to freeze-frame the moment that Thomas realises Jesus is alive, and ask: what does it tell us?

To help us ground that in real-life experience, I also got in touch with friends and contacts from a range of different backgrounds and asked them to share a bit about their journey of coming to believe in Jesus and the difference the resurrection makes to them. With their help, we're going to explore how the resurrection answers three of the most important questions we could ever ask: What is God like? Am I loved as I really am? And what happens when I die?

What Is God Like?

Thomas reacted to seeing Jesus alive again by crying out, "My Lord and my God!" He seems to realise instantly that if Jesus has defeated death, that vindicates the huge claims he had been making about himself all along. Thomas is not just looking at a good man or a prophet. Jesus is God in the flesh.

If you have read John's biography of Jesus up to this point, the conclusion Thomas comes to makes a lot of sense. As we go through everything Jesus teaches about who he is, a fascinating picture emerges. Jesus is presenting himself as God, but he also talks about God as his own Father, and also as a Spirit whom he will send into the world after he's gone. Jesus also makes it very clear that he, the Father and the Spirit are all ultimately one being—the one true God.[51] This is what Christians call "the Trinity". According to Jesus, God is one perfect being who exists in three Persons—the Father, the Son and the Spirit—who relate in perfect, overflowing love. Jesus says that he is God the Son, who has always existed since before the creation of the universe, but who has now chosen to come to earth, be born as a baby and live a real human life. Therefore, if we look at him, we see what God is really like.[52] The Bible calls Jesus "the image of the invisible God".[53]

The Trinity can be a confusing concept to wrap your head around, but here's my point: if Jesus rose from the dead, then his teaching about himself can be trusted—and that tells us a huge amount about what God is like. First it means that God isn't just a distant force or an abstract moral principle. He is infinite and transcendent, totally mind-blowing, but he's also genuinely personal. He knows us, and we can know him—not just theoretically but relationally. He is not beyond our reach.

Andre is a dad, a personal trainer, and a generally great guy to be around; he became a Christian as a 30-year-old lorry driver. His life was being ripped apart by addiction, anxiety and depression. One night, as he cried on the floor, he found himself praying and asking God for help. That prayer ultimately led him to discover Jesus and completely changed his life. Andre said this:

> I always thought: "I know there's a God, but he's so far off that he's not going to bother about me." But how very wrong I was. When I gave my life to Jesus, I knew that I was *fully known*. The Bible says that with Jesus we can be adopted as God's children. What a beautiful realisation that little old me would be known and loved by the Creator of the Universe.

Jesus doesn't just show us that God is personal; he also shows us what kind of person God is. Jesus is "the image of the invisible God"—so as we read through the biographies of Jesus' life, we are seeing the character of our Creator.

I have a friend whose whole self-understanding was transformed when she read through the Gospels and looked at the way Jesus treated women. As she saw again and again how he valued and honoured women, how utterly safe they were with him, how he forgave them for their failures and taught them the truth, it dawned on her: this is who *God* is; this is how God relates to *me*. It's an experiment worth trying yourself: just read through John's Gospel, or any of the others, and consider, what do you make of Jesus? What do you think of the way he confronts the self-righteous, embraces the outcasts, weeps with the hurting, and turns gallons of water into fine wine for a wedding? Is he what you imagined God would be like?

Am I Loved as I Really Am?

The second question gets even more personal. All of us want to know that we are loved. We want someone to truly see us—not just the masks we wear or the performance we put on but the real us—and still love us completely. But can we really be known and loved like that? We find an answer to that question in the wounds on Jesus' hands. When we grasp their significance, those wounds tell us something about ourselves that's both uncomfortable and profoundly beautiful.

Alison is a historian who was raised an atheist but

started engaging with the evidence for the resurrection at university. Looking back to when she began to be convinced, she described her thought process like this:

> The problem is, if the resurrection is true, then that drags everything else along with it. It would mean that there was a God. It would mean that the cross was necessary in order to forgive me. It would mean that—and this was a proposal which had never seemed very convincing to me before—I must not be a very good person, so that I was in need of forgiveness.

I love her honesty. There is something very confronting about a risen Jesus with nail marks in his hands, because the resurrection proves that his death wasn't a tragic accident: it was intentional. Those wounds are there for a reason; and the reason is *us*.

Jesus said that he died willingly out of love for us. He said he had come "to give his life as a ransom for many".[54] In other words, every human being is like a captive who needs to be freed—and Jesus' death paid the ransom that makes freedom possible.

In what sense are we captives? According to Jesus, we are trapped by what the Bible calls sin. That means we mess up, we do wrong things, we hurt others and we ignore God. And Jesus said that "everyone who sins is a slave to sin".[55] We're stuck, unable to escape from the guilt of our sin or its deadly consequences—except that we *can* escape, because Jesus offered his own life to be the ransom that buys our freedom! Seeing the crucified Jesus alive again tells us that, if we trust him, he really has dealt with our guilt. We can be fully forgiven and truly free—free to change and grow into the people he made us to be.

If I'm honest, like Alison, a big part of me doesn't like the idea that Jesus had to die to forgive me. I really don't like being shown that I'm not as good a person as I'd thought. Whenever a friend tells me something I've done wrong, I find myself snapping at them—desperate to show that I wasn't wrong at all, or that I had a great excuse! Most of us believe on some level that we will only be loved and accepted if we're "good enough", so whether we realise it or not, we're constantly making the case for our own defence. We spend our lives trying to convince ourselves and everyone else that we're good people—bottling up the thoughts and feelings we don't want anyone to see. We focus on how other people wrong us and ignore how we've wronged them. It's exhausting. But the nail-wounds in Jesus' hands undercut all our efforts at self-justification—and show us we don't need them.

Jesus tells us that our normal standards for being "a good person" are in fact far too low. He says what we're made for is to "Love the Lord your God with all your heart and with all your soul and with all your mind and with all your strength"—in other words, to love God with *everything you have*, since it's all a gift from him—and to "Love your neighbour as yourself", i.e. to love everyone around you *just as much as* you love yourself, since every human is just as precious to God as you are.[56]

Those are huge, deep callings. When we hear Jesus' teaching, our instinct is to say that it's not realistic.

The bar is too high—we're only human! But Jesus didn't just teach it; he lived it. He was human too, yet in his every interaction he showed us what a truly good person looks like. Personally, when I stop comparing myself with the worst bits of the people around me and start comparing myself with the courage, compassion, generosity and justice of Jesus, I realise I have a very long way to go.

But those nail-wounds mean that Jesus sees all our failures and selfishness *and loves us anyway*. He loves us so much that he willingly died in agony to forgive us. We don't have to be "good enough" to be loved and accepted. God knows you're a mess. And he thinks you're worth dying for.

Shirley became a Christian in her late fifties, after several years of reading the Bible and discussing her questions with Christian friends. I asked her what difference it makes to know that Jesus died for her, and she said:

> It is overwhelming, heartbreaking and totally humbling. I no longer feel alone and I know I'm loved—the change is palpable. I feel as though I'm becoming the me I should be.

Here's how my friend Joanna from Trinidad describes the difference it's made to how she sees herself:

> Following Jesus means knowing that no matter what, you are deeply loved and valuable to the one person who never changes. As a black woman, it's been hard to see myself as beautiful or valuable, because beauty standards in the

> world are usually focused on people with lighter skin and different features. So finding Jesus, who said that I'm deeply loved and valuable and beautiful to him, was just very deeply healing and restorative.

This kind of love means we don't need to hide or pretend. Jesus offers to take all our guilt and shame away from us for ever and make it his own—to lift our burden onto his shoulders and let it crush him instead of us. Then he offers to clothe us in his goodness and moral beauty so that we never need to be ashamed again but can come to God knowing we're accepted and adopted as his loved children—with nothing to hide, nothing to prove, and nothing to lose.

My friend Ellie expresses this beautifully. She's starting out as a doctor, and discovered Jesus a few years ago. She said:

> Before I became a Christian, I found my worth and meaning in things I had to work for and be better at—I had to continually strive to be enough. But when I trusted in Jesus, I knew my worth was found in him. I didn't have to be enough. He makes me perfect in God's eyes. It gives me so much peace to know that my identity is secure in him, and I don't have to strive anymore.

The resurrection tells us that Jesus *had* to die for us—which means we are far more in need of forgiveness than we thought. But it also tells us that Jesus was *glad* to die for us—which means we are more deeply loved and valued than we could ever have dared imagine.

What Happens When I Die?

The final thing I want us to dwell on about the risen Jesus is that he was physically, tangibly there. He invited Thomas to touch him. On another occasion he asked for some fish and ate it to prove he wasn't some kind of ghost. Another time, he cooked breakfast for his friends.[57] And this tells us something wonderful about the future he's offering us.

If we trust him, Jesus promises to bring us through death and give us a resurrection body like his in a restored world.[58] He is going to make all things new, including me.[59] That's a very different future to the one I used to imagine.

I don't know if I got it from going to a church school, or just from watching *The Simpsons* or adverts for Philadelphia cheese, but I grew up with the idea that Jesus said I could go to "heaven", which was basically sitting around on clouds playing harps. I thought my body would die and stay in the ground but my soul—a kind of ghost version of me—would drift up to an immaterial realm of vague God-ish-ness. It all sounded, if I'm honest, quite boring.

I love this physical world. I love it when the sun shines on your back and you can feel it warming you. I love it when something makes you laugh so hard, you lose control completely. I love the bright sweetness of mango. I love hugs.

But the great news is that if Jesus rose *physically* from the dead, he isn't offering us a floaty future without hugs or tastebuds—he's inviting us to join him in a resurrected world. What I'm waiting for now is a new, healed, awesome body in a world that is rich and radiant and *real*.[60] There is nothing remotely boring about that! It's everything that is precious and thrilling about life as we know it, but with all the pain and imperfection washed away; it's a life that will be saturated with the life-giving presence of an infinitely creative God!

Open Arms

It's important to be honest here: I've talked about two very different types of truth in this chapter. If Jesus rose from the dead, then he is what God is like and he loves us enough to die for us. That's just the reality, whether we realise it or not. But the forgiveness that we see in Jesus' nail-scarred hands is different, and so is the future hope I've been talking about. These are not just facts for us to discover; they are an offer that Jesus is making to us. They are not automatic. Jesus stands in front of us, like he did with Thomas, arms wide open; but what happens next is our responsibility. We can accept his offer or we can reject it. We can give him our guilt or we can keep it ourselves. We can hold him at arms' length if we want to. Or we can follow him into a whole new life.

FOR REFLECTION OR CONVERSATION

- *Look back at the three questions explored in this chapter. Which feels most significant to you?*
- *How do you feel about Jesus' answer?*

CHAPTER 6

WHAT HAPPENS NEXT

You're in the middle of Jerusalem, six weeks after Jesus of Nazareth's execution, and you're packed into a huge, jostling, murmuring crowd, peering over people's shoulders to see this guy Peter. He's speaking as loud as he can, in a thick North Galilean accent, about Jesus.

He says that God had vouched for Jesus through the miracles he did, and then he was nailed to a cross and killed, which was also part of God's plan. But then, he says, God raised him up again, freeing him from the agony of death, because it was impossible for death to keep its hold on him! He says the Scriptures promised this would happen, and now it has. "God has raised this Jesus to life, and we are all witnesses of it!" he shouts, gesturing around at the others stood behind him.[61]

When he stops talking, there's a strange hush in the crowd—tense, thoughtful. Then a voice from behind you calls out, "Brothers, what shall we do?"

It's a good question, isn't it? What does the resurrected Jesus ask of us? If he really is alive, what are we meant to do about it?

It takes a lifetime to answer that question in full colour, but in this chapter I want to just scribble you a quick sketch on a napkin with three things. Lose control; join the family; and live for what will last.

Lose Control

On that day in Jerusalem, Peter answered the "what shall we do?" question like this:

> Repent and be baptised, every one of you, in the name of Jesus Christ for the forgiveness of your sins. And you will receive the gift of the Holy Spirit.[62]

It might be hard to recognise it behind the unfamiliar language, but this answer is both radical and relational. Peter doesn't offer some moral precepts to follow or spiritual practices to try; he is essentially saying, "Give yourself to Jesus and let him restart your life."

He challenges the crowd to "repent"—which means to change your mind and turn away from your old life—and "be baptised" in the name of Jesus as a way of receiving the forgiveness he offers. Baptism is a symbolic act where you are immersed in water and then lifted out again; it's a public, physical way of saying that you want Jesus and everything he's done to be *yours*. You don't just want it to be theoretical or cultural; you want it to be personal.

It's actually a lot like a wedding ceremony.

As we exchanged rings on our wedding day, Rachael and I said to each other, "All that I am I give to you; all that I have I share with you." As we gave ourselves to one another, we were united permanently. Our old single lives were over, and everything we had was shared. All her student debts became my student debts; my crazy Northern Irish family became her crazy Northern Irish family! And that's exactly how the Bible says it is with us and Jesus.

Jesus got down on one knee to us as he died on the cross. To put our faith in him is to realise that and simply say "Yes". Then baptism is like the wedding ceremony, where Jesus says to us, "All that I am I give to you; all that I have I share with you" and we say it back. Our old single life is over and everything we have is shared! We belong to Jesus now—so our debt of guilt becomes his debt, our death becomes his death, and he deals with it all for ever on the cross. And Jesus belongs to us! His Father becomes our Father, his family becomes our family and his life becomes our life.

This is why the symbolism of plunging down into water and then rising back up again is so powerful. It's like we're giving Jesus our old life, asking him to bury it under the water and raise us up to a new life with him. That's why Peter says we will "receive the gift of the Holy Spirit": when we're united to Jesus, God the Holy Spirit comes to live in us and transform us. Jesus shares his new life with us from the inside out.

I'll be honest, this is a pretty daunting prospect—because, as with getting married, it means you're just not in control anymore. A healthy marriage means putting the other person first. It means not being independent: there is someone now who isn't you and doesn't always agree with you, but who you care about more than yourself. Repenting and giving yourself to Jesus is like that. My life isn't about me anymore. I'm living for him—I care about him more than I care about myself, and he's a real person who definitely doesn't always agree with me. I've willingly given up control.

But just as with marriage, that's not just frightening; it's thrilling. We surrender control to Jesus because we know he genuinely wants what's best for us and he's infinitely wiser than we are. Jesus once said, "Whoever wants to be my disciple must deny themselves and take up their cross and follow me." But he also said, "I have come that [you] may have life, and have it to the full."[63] That's not a contradiction. According to Jesus, "denying yourself" to put him first is actually the way to come fully alive. The way to find yourself is to follow him.

It sounds paradoxical, but we can trust that it's true. Jesus has already surrendered his own life for us—so we know he is utterly committed to our good. And he's risen again—so he knows the way to real life.

My friend Rob wrestled with the question of Jesus for a couple of years before he started to follow him. Here's his experience:

> When I look back at the way I used to live, I have no regrets on "missing out" on that by choosing to honour God with my life now—what he offers us is so much better ... Jesus is the source of life, so following him isn't so much denial of self

> (although it involves that) as much as renewal and retrieval of self—alive in the person God intended me to be.

I love that. Jesus is the one who made us. So giving up control and letting him take the lead is the way to discover who we really are. It's how we become the person we were made to be.

But we're not meant to attempt that journey on our own.

Join the Family

Christianity is all about relationships.

Naushin grew up in a devout Muslim family, but she discovered Jesus in her late teens and at university, and it's been fascinating to hear how different her experience has been since then:

> When I became a Christian I was constantly amazed by how much an ancient book [the Bible] could be relevant to my everyday life, and how it could bring comfort. I was amazed that God has not left us alone to our devices and our pain. The image of God as a father tenderly lifting the downcast out of the ash heap is one that has brought me great comfort in times of suffering.[64] This was a huge contrast to how I related to God before, as a distant being whose approval or disapproval I couldn't fathom.

Rhydhm came to the UK to study, having grown up in northern India. Christianity was entirely foreign to her—until a series of chance encounters in some of her darkest moments led her to investigate who Jesus really was. Here's how she describes what it's been like to start following him:

> I had a really rough childhood. After being with Christ all I can say is that I have hope, and courage which no doctor or medicine was able to give me before. I feel I have a father figure who is reshaping me into a better adult. Someone is there to look after and listen and guide me ... Following Jesus is like you are never alone. He gives us a home, which is church, and a family, which is our church community. Jesus answers my most pressing questions—sometimes through Sunday church services or sometimes through reading the Bible with a friend. He always answers your prayers and you see those evidences in your life. Ever since I've been with Christ there are a lot of coincidences in my life!

I love how emphatically relational those descriptions are. Jesus brings us into a new family: he brings us to God as our Father, so we can talk to him freely through prayer and hear him speak to us in the Bible, and he surrounds us with brothers and sisters in the church.

This is exactly what happened after Peter told that crowd about Jesus. Around 3,000 people accepted his invitation and got baptised, and immediately they joined the communal life of their new family. "They devoted themselves to the apostles' teaching and to fellowship, to the breaking of bread and to prayer."[65]

In other words, their new life wasn't some elusive, floaty thing—sitting alone and trying to summon up a spiritual state of mind. It was a profoundly human thing: they engaged their minds, hearts and bodies in a new life together, caring for each other, actively learning and enjoying the truth about Jesus and interacting with him in prayer.

Chia-Wen grew up in a Buddhist home in China and is only just starting out in life with Jesus. Here's his description:

> I like the Christian life in practice, which includes worship, Bible studies, and praying. Those activities are very healthy for human beings—they definitely improve our mental health ... I am a beginner in learning Christ, so things and stories in the Bible are new to me, and I question when I read the Bible. I appreciate brothers and sisters in the church who always love to answer my questions and deeply discuss with me.

What this adds up to is that exploring what it means to follow Jesus is surprisingly simple. Get involved in a church community that loves the Bible, and find some people there who are up for reading it with you and praying together.

Live for What Will Last

Finally, we come to one of the most wonderful things about Jesus' resurrection. Not only does Jesus offer us a life of unimaginable joy beyond death, he also invites us to live lives now, before death, that really *matter*. He is calling you to a life of eternal significance.

My friend Joanna told me this was really precious to her:

> I have always been very aware of my mortality and so often found most things pointless. Why should I "do good" just for the sake of it, if it wasn't going to matter when I died and if others didn't live the same way? Christianity was the only thing that told me I was inherently valuable and could have a deeper purpose beyond this life: the opportunity to join in the eternal work that God was already doing.

Life can be so frustrating, can't it? Do you ever, like Joanna, end up asking, *what's the point?* We work so hard but most of the time our efforts feel painfully temporary. It's like we're building beautiful sandcastles on the beach, but the tide is creeping closer and closer. Everything we are and everything we've ever done will be forgotten before too long. The average grave gets visited for just 15 years, and after a hundred no one will remember us at all. Everything we've achieved will get ruined or replaced. The tide keeps coming until eventually there's nothing left. Until none of it seems to matter.

But if we live for Jesus, things are very different. Paul, one of the witnesses of Jesus' resurrection, writes in a letter about how it was the first instalment of an eternal new world that God is making and that Christians are part of.[66] He concludes by telling us what that means for our lives right now:

> Therefore, my dear brothers and sisters, stand firm. Let nothing move you. Always give yourselves fully to the work of the Lord, because you know that your labour in the Lord is not in vain.[67]

Paul says that if we give our lives to Jesus and don't give up, we can know that our efforts *matter*. If we focus on following him, doing what he loves and contributing to his "kingdom" rather than our own, then we're not building sandcastles, we're planting seeds.

Seeds are crazy when you think about them. A seed looks tiny, dull and unimpressive to begin with, and then you bury it in the ground! The whole thing looks like a waste of time. But come back in a hundred years, and you're standing in the shade of a magnificent tree. You crane your neck back, looking up to see the sun shining through the canopy of leaves—and it takes your breath away. Planting that little seed was not a waste of time.

The resurrected Jesus invites us to participate now in the new world he has started, which means that everything we do for him is like a seed. It won't be washed away into nothingness—all death can do is plant it. Every minute of hard, honest work; every patient hour of caring for family or friends; every long year of holding onto hope in the fight with ill health—none of it will be wasted. Jesus sees it, he values it, and he will bring something precious out of it—perhaps in us, perhaps in other people, perhaps in a way we can't even imagine right now. When Jesus raises us from the dead into a healed world and wipes every tear from our eyes, we'll see what he's done with all the feeble, insignificant-looking seeds we've sown, and it will take our breath away.

Jesus is inviting us to give him control, join his family, and spend our lives on what will last for ever. Because if Jesus died for you and then rose from the dead, your life matters. He cares about you. He doesn't just want to forgive you: he wants you in his family, and he wants you in the family business, playing your part in what he's doing to bring healing, truth and hope to this weary world. It's daunting. But it will not be a waste. It will be absolutely and eternally worth it.

FOR REFLECTION OR CONVERSATION

- *What appeals to you about life with Jesus?*
- *What do you think you would find challenging?*

CONCLUSION

A FEW FINAL QUESTIONS

I wish we were sitting together in a sunny park somewhere and we could talk about what you make of all this. If you've made it this far, you'll probably have all kinds of questions that I haven't even tried to answer. But for now, let me pose a few questions of my own for you to ponder.

If you've patiently stuck with me all the way to the end but you're not yet convinced, then first of all, thank you! The open-mindedness it takes to get this far is a precious thing. I'd also love to ask you, though: if you're not convinced by Jesus, what are you believing instead? It's absolutely right to question what I've written here, but I'd invite you to also question whatever you currently believe. The resurrection may sound far-fetched—but then, if we weren't so used to it, the universe would seem far-fetched; our own consciousness would seem far-fetched; life and love and maths and music would seem far-fetched! What do you think is the best explanation for the whole magnificent mystery of existence? Or to look at it from another angle, are you sure enough that Christianity *isn't* true that you're happy betting your life on that? If not, it might just be worth doing a bit more digging.

Or if, while you've been reading this, you've felt your perspective shifting, and you think you might be beginning to believe it, can I encourage you to talk to Jesus about that? He's alive, he loves you, and he's right there with you listening. You can literally just speak to him, or you could write out a prayer like a letter. You might want to say sorry or thank you—or, to be honest, probably both. You might want to ask him to come and forgive you and be with you and restart your life. It doesn't need to be eloquent or complicated—I promise you, he's just delighted to hear your voice.

Why not talk to another Christian about it too? We're not meant to be solo explorers launching out into the spiritual jungle alone; we need our new family. So talk to someone. Start going along to a church, and persevere with it even if it seems weird to begin with. I am praying for you right now that this might be the beginning of a truly epic journey.

Finally, you might already have been convinced that Jesus rose before you started reading. If so, can I gently ask you, are you living your life on the basis that Jesus is actually alive? Have you accepted his invitation to die to yourself and discover real life with him? Are you enjoying and investing in your relationship with him and his family? Are you playing your part in what he's doing in this world, planting seeds that will last for ever? And if you feel like you're not really doing those things, what's holding you back?

We began this book with the voice of my old chemistry teacher reminding us that, whether we eat a whole cabbage or not, "Everybody dies, kids." Wonderfully, we don't have to end there.

I'd like to end instead with the voice of Jesus. He's alive, and whoever you are, he's holding out his nail-scarred hands and saying this to you:

> I am the resurrection and the life. The one who believes in me will live, even though they die.
>
> I am the good shepherd. I lay down my life for the sheep.
>
> I have come that they may have life, and have it to the full.
>
> Follow me.[68]

APPENDIX I

WHY SHOULD I TRUST WHAT THE BIBLE SAYS ABOUT JESUS?

Professor John Dickson

There is so much scepticism about the Bible today and about Jesus, in particular. But the New Testament texts describing Jesus' life, teaching, death and resurrection pass the test of history with flying colours. What follows are just four of the good reasons we have for considering the New Testament to be a reliable historical source.

1. The New Testament contains a "collection" of independent evidence about Jesus.

The New Testament seems like one book today. But, originally, many of these texts were written independently of each other.

The Gospel of Mark was written without a knowledge of what was in the letters of Paul. Paul himself wrote without any knowledge of the Gospel of Mark. James wrote his letter without possessing copies of Mark or Paul's epistles. Here, then, are three separate sources, only later (in the second century) brought into a single volume called the New Testament.

There are even sources within individual Gospels, according to most secular experts today. Luke in his opening line tells us, "Many have undertaken to draw up an account of the things that have been fulfilled among us." Today, scholars reckon they can detect at least three separate sources in his Gospel. Overall, then, there are between five and seven sources in the New Testament which haven't been simply copied from each other.

The point of the observation—from the historical point of view—is that this fulfils one of the most important "tests" that contemporary historians apply when trying to work out what happened in the past: do we have more than one source testifying to the event? In the case of Jesus, we have between five and seven different sources saying roughly the same thing about him. That puts the broad outline of Jesus' life beyond reasonable doubt for most specialists working today.

2. The New Testament sources are relatively early.

In ancient history, scholars are used to assessing sources written many decades, or even centuries, after the events under investigation. That's the norm.

Rarely, if ever, do we find sources contemporaneous with events. So, for example, our first detailed biographical account of Alexander the Great (356-323 BC) was written by Polybius about 120 years after Alexander's death. Likewise, the most important account of Emperor Tiberius, who ruled when Jesus lived, was penned by Tacitus some 80 years after his death.

The New Testament documents, on the other hand, are significantly earlier. The Gospel source known as Q and the earliest letters of Paul come from around the year 50, just 20 years after Jesus' death. Several more documents (like Mark and James) come from the 60s, just 30 or so years after Jesus. And the latest New Testament document in the opinion of secular scholars, the Gospel of John, was probably written around the year 90, just 60 years after the event. (Personally, I think John was written much earlier, but I'm giving the dates used by most secular specialists.) That means that the *latest* New Testament record we have for Jesus is still earlier than the best record we have for Emperor Tiberius who lived at the same time.

3. Even though the words and deeds of Jesus weren't written down immediately, they were carefully preserved in an oral tradition.

In the ancient world only about 10-15 percent of the population could read. So people's first instinct when important things happened wasn't to write them down. That only preserved the news for a small, elite subset of the population. If you wanted the masses to know something—whether an important military event, a summary of a philosophical system or a particular teacher's sayings—you relied on what scholars call "oral tradition".

In our instant, media-saturated world, we expect things to be on Twitter or our news feeds within minutes of them happening. But that's not how the first century worked. We know beyond doubting that ancient Greeks, Romans and Jews were well practised in the art of memorisation and rehearsal of important material. (We have lost this art, to our great detriment.)

For example, initiates in the philosophy of Epicurus, one of the most popular schools in the period, had to learn by heart about 2,000 words of complex philosophical sayings of the founder of the movement. This wasn't unusual. Jewish rabbis made similar demands of their disciples, and all the evidence points to Jesus insisting upon the same with his disciples. These disciples then appointed others—known as "teachers"—to ensure that the same material was passed on and preserved in the growing churches.

4. The New Testament is probably the best-preserved text of all ancient history.

A rumour has spread that the text of the New Testament has not been reliably passed down through the centuries. It was copied from one document to another document, translated from one dead language to another dead language, and eventually it ended up in our pew Bibles. Who knows if what we read today is what the original writers first wrote!?

Well, in fact we do know. The more manuscript copies of an ancient text we have, the better able we are to determine what was in the original document. Mistakes and changes certainly happen—in all ancient copies of documents—but if you only have, say, two or three copies of a document and they vary from one another here and there, it is quite difficult to work out which wording is original and which is a variation.

So how does the New Testament fare in the copying stakes? Better than any other ancient writing! Let me offer the fairest comparison imaginable. The most celebrated epic poem of Roman history is the *Aeneid*, by Virgil (it runs about the same length as the four Gospels combined). It was so popular, it was copied over and over. And it is now considered the best-preserved Latin text we have from ancient times. It has come down to us in the following manuscript copies:

- Three complete or near-complete copies
- Seven partial manuscripts (a partial manuscript could include 50 or more pages of writing)
- 20 papyrus fragments (which might just be a page or two)

Compare this with the New Testament manuscript copies:

- Four complete or near-complete copies (very comparable to the *Aeneid*)
- 340 partial manuscripts (far more than the *Aeneid*. And keep in mind that "partial" can include manuscripts which contain entire Gospels or several of Paul's letters)
- 1,000s of papyrus fragments (scraps of paper with short or long passages from the New Testament)

Because of the overwhelming number of copies of the New Testament, we are far more easily able to spot the variations and arrive at a high degree of confidence about the original text.

John Dickson is Jean Kvamme Distinguished Professor of Biblical Studies and Public Christianity at Wheaton College in Illinois.

This appendix is an edited extract from an article called "10 Reasons You Can Trust the Bible", originally published on 1 March, 2017 on eternitynews.com.au. You can read the full text here: undeceptions.com/media/10-reasons-you-can-trust-the-bible

APPENDIX II

SCIENCE OR FAITH?

Professor John C. Lennox

I am often told that the trouble with believers in God is just that: *they are believers*. That is, they are people of faith. Science is far superior because it doesn't require faith. It sounds great. The problem is, it could not be more wrong.

Many atheists think that faith is a religious concept that means *believing where you know there is no evidence*. They are quite wrong. The word faith comes from the Latin *fides*, which means loyalty or trust. And, if we have any sense, we don't normally trust facts or people without evidence. After all, making well-motivated, evidence-based *decisions* is just how faith is normally exercised—think of how you get your bank manager to trust you or the basis for your decision to get on board a bus or an aircraft.

Believing where there is no evidence is what is usually called *blind faith*. I cannot speak for other religions, but the faith expected on the part of Christians is certainly not blind. I would have no interest in it otherwise.

Do Atheists Have Faith?

This confusion about the nature of faith leads many people to another serious error: thinking that neither atheism nor science involves faith. Yet, the irony is that science cannot do without faith.

Physicist Paul Davies points out that "even the most atheistic scientist accepts *as an act of faith* [emphasis mine] ... a law-like order in nature that is at least in part comprehensible to us".[69] Albert Einstein famously said:

> To [the sphere of religion] there also belongs the faith in the possibility that the regulations valid for the world of existence are rational, that is, comprehensible to reason. *I cannot conceive a genuine man of science without that profound faith* [emphasis mine]. The situation may be expressed by an image: science without religion is lame, religion without science is blind.[70]

Einstein evidently did not suffer from the delusion that all faith is blind faith. Einstein speaks of the "profound faith" of the scientist in the rational intelligibility of the universe. He could not imagine a scientist without it.

Why Is the Universe Intelligible to Reason?

My lecturer in quantum mechanics at Cambridge, Professor Sir John Polkinghorne, wrote, "Science does not explain the mathematical intelligibility of the physical world, for it is part of science's founding *faith* [notice his explicit use of the word] that this is so..." for the simple reason that you cannot begin to do physics without believing in that intelligibility.[71]

On what evidence do scientists base their faith in the rational intelligibility of the universe, which allows them to do science? The first thing to notice is that *human reason did not create the universe*. This point is so obvious that at first it might seem trivial; but it is, in fact, of fundamental importance when we come to assess the validity of our cognitive faculties. Not only did we not create the universe, but we did not create our own powers of reason either. We can develop our rational faculties by use; but we did not originate them. How can it be, then, that what goes on in our tiny heads can give us anything near a true account of reality? How can it be that a mathematical equation thought up in the mind of a mathematician can correspond to the workings of the universe?

It was this very question that led Einstein to say, "The most incomprehensible thing about the world is that it is comprehensible". Similarly the Nobel Prize winning physicist Eugene Wigner once wrote a famous paper entitled, "The unreasonable effectiveness of mathematics in the natural sciences". But it is only unreasonable from an atheistic perspective. From the biblical point of view, it resonates perfectly.

Why Do We Have Faith in Our Own Brains?

Sometimes, when in conversation with my fellow scientists, I ask them "What do you do science with?"

"My mind," say some, and others, who hold the view that the mind is the brain, say, "My brain".

"Tell me about your brain? How does it come to exist?"

"By means of natural, mindless, unguided processes."

"Why, then, do you trust it?" I ask. "If you thought that your computer was the end product of mindless unguided processes, would you trust it?"

"Not in a million years," comes the reply.

"You clearly have a problem then."

After a pregnant pause they sometimes ask me where I got this argument—they find the answer rather surprising: Charles Darwin. He wrote:

> ...with me the horrid doubt always arises whether the convictions of man's mind, which has been developed from the mind of the lower animals, are of any value or at all trustworthy.[72]

Atheism Undermines Rationality

Taking the obvious logic of this statement further, physicist John Polkinghorne says that if you reduce mental events to physics and chemistry you destroy meaning. How?

> For thought is replaced by electrochemical neural events ... The world of rational discourse disappears into the absurd chatter of firing synapses. Quite frankly that can't be right and none of us believe it to be so.[73]

Another leading philosopher, Thomas Nagel, thinks in the same way. He has written a book, *Mind and Cosmos*, with the provocative subtitle *Why the Neo-Darwinian View of the World is Almost Certainly False*. Nagel is a strong atheist who says with some honesty, "I don't want there to be a God". And yet he writes:

> But if the mental is not itself merely physical, it cannot be fully explained by physical science. Evolutionary naturalism implies that we shouldn't take any of our convictions seriously, including the scientific world picture on which evolutionary naturalism itself depends.[74]

That is, naturalism, and therefore atheism, undermines the foundations of the very rationality that is needed to construct or understand or believe in any kind of argument whatsoever, let alone a scientific one.

C.S. Lewis observes:

> The Naturalists have been engaged in thinking about Nature. They have not attended to the fact that they were thinking. The moment one attends to this it is obvious that one's own thinking cannot be merely a natural event, and therefore something other than Nature exists.[75]

Not only does science fail to rule out the supernatural—the very doing of science or any other rational activity rules it in. The Bible gives us a reason for trusting reason. Atheism does not.

John C. Lennox is Emeritus Professor of Mathematics at the University of Oxford and the author of many books.

This article is an edited extract from his book "Can Science Explain Everything?"

APPENDIX III

AREN'T ALL RELIGIONS EQUALLY VALID?

Piyush Jani

As someone who was born in a Hindu household but is now a Christian, this is a question I have been asked many times.

It is a natural question to ask for those of us living in today's multicultural society. Our exposure to different religions has increased. We are surrounded by mosques, temples and synagogues as well as churches. We live and work with people of different faiths. One of my neighbours is a Buddhist, while the other is Jewish; they have become my friends.

Despite differences, there is generally a desire to work together for a cohesive society. We rightly want to live at peace, respecting the different cultures and religious beliefs of those around us and working together for the common good. In this atmosphere of respect and tolerance, many start to think that all religions should be considered as equally valid—just as true as one another.

This is actually a very academic and Western thought—it is only common where adherents of religion are relatively few. In the rest of the world, where adherence to religion is more widespread, the idea that all religions can be harmonised would be rejected. I remember listening to a panel discussion once between a Jewish rabbi, a Muslim imam and a Christian minister. They each respectfully disagreed with the others and claimed that theirs was the true faith. To give another striking example, if my friend's Muslim father, who has disowned his son for converting to Christianity, were told that all religions are the same, he would be deeply offended!

This is not surprising, because even the briefest study of the world's religions will reveal far more contradictions than consensus. For example, the conception of God (Allah in Islam, Brahma in Hinduism, and Yahweh in the Hebrew scriptures) is so very different. Buddhism, in its classic formulation, is atheistic with no God. As another example, the major religions offer very different responses to the important topics of sin, suffering and death.

Speaking personally, if all religions were equally valid, then I would have had no reason to convert from Hinduism to Christianity. So, what was it about Christianity that was so different that it led me to convert? It was the person of Jesus.

The Distinctiveness of Jesus

When as a Hindu I read the New Testament, several distinctive Christian beliefs became unmistakably clear:

- That Jesus claims to be the unique revelation of God.
- That he claims to be the exclusive way of salvation which can be found nowhere else.
- That he is the only way to reconciliation with God.

Jesus categorically stated about himself:

> I am the way and the truth and the life. No one comes to [God] the Father except through me.[76]

His followers understood this and soon began to proclaim that salvation is found in no one else, "for there is no other name under heaven given to mankind by which we must be saved".[77]

This led me to realise two things:

1. Jesus is unique amongst all other religious leaders.

In Islam, Muhammad never claimed to be divine, but instead pointed toward Allah. To a Muslim, the Quran is of primary importance rather than Muhammad.

When the Buddha was asked near his death how it would be best to remember him, he told his followers not to bother with such a silly question. What is important, he said, is not himself but his teaching.

In Hinduism, deities are considered different aspects or manifestations of the ultimate reality, Brahma.

The New Testament, on the other hand, clearly depicts Jesus Christ as fully divine. Jesus is portrayed as the "image" or "the exact representation" of God.[78] Remarkably, Jesus himself stated that to have seen him is to have seen God the Father.[79] Even those who rejected him understood his claim and protested that he was "making himself equal with God"; others, who acknowledged Jesus, fell on their knees in front of him and exclaimed "My Lord and my God!".[80]

This claim is without parallel. No other major religious leaders have claimed to be God himself.

2. The message of Christianity is unique amongst all other religious messages.

All religions other than Christianity are in essence full of counsel and advice. They inform us that we should live in a certain way so that we may find our way to God. They tell us that the way to God depends on our own endeavours and efforts. If our lives are good enough, if our self-control is rigorous enough, if our devotions are fervent and if our faith is zealous, then perhaps we may see God.

Jesus knows this can never be the case. According to Christianity, by our own efforts we can never be moral enough to come into the presence of God. Here, instead of advice and counsel, we are offered an invitation. Jesus invites us to come to him—just as we are, wherever we are, and whatever we have done. Other religions tell us what we need to do, but Christianity says that the work is all done!

Christianity alone dares to claim that the all-knowing, all-powerful God uniquely intervened in his creation—and not just by living and teaching, but by dying a criminal's death for us and for our salvation. We simply need to receive salvation as an undeserved gift.

My Conversion and My Confidence

I came to realise that no matter how zealous my faith was or how fervent my devotions, these could never make up for my dark and sinful heart. Hinduism kept saying, "Try harder," but offered no solutions for my karma (the consequence of my sins). By contrast, in Christianity, God himself reveals both the nature of my sin as it really is and also his incredible love which took him to the cross to deal with my sin.

When I understood this invitation, I realized that there can be no other way. I accepted Jesus' offer of free and full forgiveness, receiving mercy rather than judgement.

So, what is my life like now as a Christian?

First, I am confident that my sins have been forgiven (1 Corinthians 15:3-4). My *past* is dealt with.

Second, I live day by day in God's power. The same power which raised Christ from the dead is at work in my life (Ephesians 1:19-20). I have resources to love God and my neighbour. Therefore, I have help to live in the *present*.

Third, I do not fear death or judgement (John 5:4; Romans 8:1). Christ has overcome sin and death. Therefore, there is now no condemnation for those who belong to Christ. Jesus has promised to save me completely and forever. My *future* is secure.

Why am I so confident? Partly because there is so much evidence that the resurrection of Jesus Christ took place in history. This evidence may be helpful for those who are not Christians and are not yet convinced that Jesus is divine. But this historical fact of Jesus' resurrection from the dead is also of first importance to Christians—providing us with deep assurance that Jesus' promises to act on our behalf are trustworthy.

This is why I no longer follow the Hindu tradition I was raised with. I worship a Saviour who was crucified and has risen again, and he has my past, present and future completely covered.

Piyush Jani is a consultant surgeon at Cambridge University Hospital. He was born in Kenya and grew up in a Hindu household.

APPENDIX IV

FURTHER READING

I hope you've reached the end of this book with more questions than you had to begin with. Here are a few ideas of things you might find helpful and interesting after a book like this.

1. Read the Bible itself

In this book I've used the NIV (New International Version) which is a great translation into modern English. You might want to start with John's Gospel, which we've explored a little bit in this book. Some other great places to start would be...

- Luke's Gospel, followed by Acts. Luke talked to various eyewitnesses to write a biography of Jesus, and then a history of how Christianity as a movement began after Jesus' resurrection.
- Paul's letters, such as Philippians or Colossians—these give a great snapshot of who Jesus is and what difference it makes to know him and follow him.

- The Psalms in the Old Testament are a collection of songs and prayers that God's people used up to the time of Jesus and then beyond. They are an honest and beautiful introduction to how we are invited to talk to God.

You might want to use some resources to help you understand and enjoy what you're reading:

- The *God's Word For You* series has great, engaging notes with reflection questions.
- The Bible Project is a YouTube channel with loads of great videos, especially their overviews of books of the Bible, that can help you get a grip on what's going on in the Bible book you want to read.
- *The Quiet Time Kickstart* by Rachel Jones is a kind of couch-to-5K style introduction to reading a little bit of the Bible and praying about it each day, helping you develop a life-giving habit over six weeks.

2. Watch some videos

If you want something to help you get your head around the fundamentals of Christianity a bit more deeply, I'd recommend the free video course at 321course.com. It has eight thought-provoking and enjoyable short videos.

3. Find out more about the resurrection

If you want to take a deep dive into the historical evidence for the resurrection, the two most significant books to get your hands on are these:

- *The Resurrection of Jesus: A New Historiographical Approach*, Michael Licona
- *The Resurrection of the Son of God*, N.T. Wright
- And if you'd like to read a thoughtful sceptical view of things from a non-Christian scholar alongside those for comparison, you could try *The Resurrection* by Géza Vermes.
- Finally, for more exploration of what the Bible teaches about the difference Jesus' resurrection makes to us today, I'd recommend *Life After Life* by Mark Meynell.

4. Explore other important questions

- *Why God Makes Sense in a World That Doesn't*, Gavin Ortlund—exploring more philosophically whether we have good reason to believe that God actually exists.
- *Confronting Christianity*, Rebecca McLaughlin—exploring twelve of the most common objections to Christianity in the modern world.
- *Seeking Allah, Finding Jesus* and *No God But One*, Nabeel Qureshi—comparing the claims of Islam and Christianity from first-hand experience.
- *The Air We Breathe*, Glen Scrivener—considering the moral values most of us hold dear, and showing how our society learned them from Jesus.

- *Walking With God Through Pain and Suffering*, Tim Keller—asking how we can believe in a loving God in the midst of suffering and evil, and how to walk with him through it.
- *Unbreakable: What the Son of God Said about the Word of God*, Andrew Wilson—exploring what Jesus believed and taught about the Bible and what that means for our relationship with it today.
- *What It Means to Be Protestant*, Gavin Ortlund—considering the claims of different branches of the church (Protestant, Catholic and Eastern Orthodox) to be faithful to the true message of Jesus.

And of course, much better than reading by yourself would be finding a church that loves Jesus and loves the Bible and helps you get to grips with it in community. If you don't know where to find a church like that near you, or you have any questions that you're not sure how to find an answer to, or you'd just like to let me know your thoughts about the book, I'd love to hear from you at theifthatchangeseverything@gmail.com.

NOTES

Chapter 1

1 "'Hope Is a Powerful Weapon': Unpublished Mandela Prison Letters" (New York Times, 6 Jul. 2018): nytimes.com/2018/07/06/opinion/sunday/nelson-mandela-unpublished-prison-letters-excerpts.html (accessed 4 Apr. 2025).

2 John 11:25.

3 I am indebted for this idea to Gavin Ortlund's brilliant book *Why God Makes Sense in a World That Doesn't* (Baker Academic, 2021), p. 101-107.

4 Acts 17:30-31.

5 See Matthew 25:31-33 and John 5:25-29.

6 See for example Mark 15:1-41.

7 Rachael Denhollander taught me to understand justice in these terms—see her powerful victim impact statement at the trial of Larry Nassar and her book *What Is a Girl Worth?*

8 "The Death of Evil upon the Seashore" (Sermon

at the Cathedral of St John the Divine, New York, 17 May 1956): kinginstitute.stanford.edu/king-papers/documents/death-evil-upon-seashore-sermon-delivered-service-prayer-and-thanksgiving (accessed 11 Apr. 2025).

9 1 Corinthians 15:14-15.

Chapter 2

10 Ted Honderich, *The Oxford Companion to Philosophy* (Oxford University Press, Second Edition, 2005), p. 434.

11 I am indebted for this illustration to Andrew Wilson in *If God, Then What?* (IVP, 2012), p. 31-47.

12 Stephen Hawking, *A Brief History of Time* (Bantam, 1988), p. 174.

13 Paul Davies, *The Mind of God* (Simon & Schuster, 1992), p. 49-50.

14 Ian Hutchinson, *Can a Scientist Believe in Miracles?* (IVP, 2018), p. 122.

15 Larry Sanger, "How a Skeptical Philosopher Becomes a Christian" (5 Feb. 2025): larrysanger.org/2025/02/how-a-skeptical-philosopher-becomes-a-christian (accessed 11 Apr. 2025), emphasis mine.

16 Francis Crick, *Life Itself* (MacDonald, 1982), p. 88.

17 Francis Crick with L.E. Orgel, "Directed Panspermia" (*Icarus*, Vol. 19, Issue 3, Jul. 1973): www.sciencedirect.com/science/article/pii/0019103573901103 (accessed 16 Apr. 2025).

18 That's in a 2022 UK survey called *Talking Jesus*: eauk.org/assets/files/downloads/Talking-Jesus-Report.pdf, p. 8 (accessed 11 Apr. 2025). For comparable

surveys in Australia and the US, see ncls.org.au/articles/australians-views-of-god-and-jesus and thestateoftheology.com (both accessed 11 Apr. 2025).

19 E.g. Luke 5:17-26.

20 Matthew 25:31-33 and John 5:24-27.

21 John 8:58 and 17:24.

22 John 14:5-9.

23 C.S. Lewis, *Mere Christianity* (Collins, 2012), p. 52.

Chapter 3

24 John Dominic Crossan, *Who Killed Jesus?* (HarperSanFrancisco, 1995), p. 5.

25 Josephus, *Antiquities of the Jews* 18.3.3 and Tacitus, *Annals* 15.44—works of history written just before and just after 100 AD respectively.

26 N.T. Wright, *The Resurrection of the Son of God* (SPCK, 2003), p. 558-563.

27 See p. 611-616 in Timothy & Lydia McGrew, "The Argument From Miracles", in *The Blackwell Companion to Natural Theology*, ed. William Lane Craig and J.P. Moreland, (Blackwell Publishing, 2012); also Rodney Stark, *The Rise of Christianity* (Princeton University Press, 1996), p. 186.

28 Gerd Lüdemann with Alf Özen, trans. John Bowdon, *What Really Happened to Jesus?* (SCM Press, 1995), p. 80.

29 See 1 Corinthians 15:1-7; Acts 26:1-29.

30 For example Clement of Rome, *1 Clement* 5 (c. 95 AD); Ignatius of Antioch, *Epistle to the Ephesians* 12.2 (c. 110-115 AD); Peter of Alexandria, *Canonical Epistle* 9 (306 AD); and Eusebius, *Ecclesiastical*

History 2.25.1-8 (c. 320 AD), who references earlier accounts of Paul's death from Dionysius of Corinth in the mid-100s AD and Tertullian in c. 200 AD.

31 See Michael Licona, *The Resurrection of Jesus: A New Historiographical Approach* (Apollos, 2010), p. 460-461.

32 For example Galatians (Turkey), 1 Thessalonians and 1 Corinthians (Greece), and Romans (Italy).

33 Tacitus, *Annals* 15.44.

34 Dr Jim Paul explains: "The loss of blood volume and dehydration caused by crucifixion resulted in such physical stress that victims would have suffered a collection of fluid around the heart (pericardial effusion) or lungs (pleural effusion) or both. Any of these would have been terminal events for a person suspended by their arms from a cross." *What on Earth Is Heaven?* (IVP, 2021), p. 100.

35 Many Muslims believe that Jesus avoided crucifixion entirely by miraculous means, but since that claim was made on theological grounds 600 years later, we can't consider it here. I would recommend Nabeel Qureshi's careful discussion in *No God But One* (Zondervan, 2016), p. 161-186.

36 Bart Ehrman in debate with Justin Bass: youtube.com/watch?v=LVUQAVQS1-U (accessed 14 Apr. 2025).

37 This would remain the situation for almost the first three centuries of the church. It wasn't until Constantine became the first Roman emperor to convert to Christianity in 312 AD that it began to be potentially advantageous to be a Christian.

38 Wright, p. 607.

39 Origen, *Against Celsus* 2.55.

40 The resurrection accounts in the four Gospels are different to each other in a way that makes it obvious they weren't copying or colluding, but is the sort of variation you get if you ask different eyewitnesses to describe one set of events and then get four different people to summarise their descriptions. I used to be concerned by the fact that the accounts aren't identical, but now I think it's actually a strong piece of evidence that they are authentic accounts of what people saw! If you'd like a scholarly deep-dive into this, take a look at Richard Bauckham's book *Jesus and the Eyewitnesses.*

41 Joseph Bergeron and Gary R. Habermas, "The Resurrection of Jesus: A Clinical Review of Psychiatric Hypotheses for the Biblical Story of Easter", *LBTS Faculty Publications and Presentations,* 2015: digitalcommons.liberty.edu/cgi/viewcontent.cgi?article=1407&context=lts_fac_pubs (accessed 14 Apr. 2025).

42 Most notably the letter 1 Corinthians.

43 One of the Ten Commandments, the original moral code in the Hebrew Bible, is "You shall not bear false witness" (see Exodus 20:16; Leviticus 19:11). For Jesus' words about truth, see for example John 18:37; John 8:31-32; John 1:17.

44 See Matthew 28; Luke 24; John 20–21; Acts 1 and 1 Corinthians 15.

Chapter 4

45 Tim Adams, "Eddie Izzard: Everything I do in life is trying to get my mother back", *The Guardian*, 10 Sep. 2017: theguardian.com/culture/2017/sep/10/eddie-izzard-trying-to-get-mother-back-victoria-and-abdul (accessed 17 Apr. 2025). Izzard is still happy to be known as Eddie and "he", but now also goes by Suzy and "she".

46 John 20:24-25.

47 Thomas Kuhn, *The Structure of Scientific Revolutions* (University of Chicago Press, second edition, 1970), p. 62-65.

48 See N.T. Wright, *The Resurrection of the Son of God* (SPCK, 2003), p. 200-206.

49 John 20:26-29, continued below.

50 "Can a historian believe in the resurrection?" *Confronting Christianity with Rebecca McLaughlin* podcast, 14 Nov. 2023.

Chapter 5

51 E.g. John 17:24; 14:8-13; 14:16-18; 10:30.

52 E.g. John 14:5-13; 6:35-40; 12:44-46.

53 Colossians 1:15.

54 Mark 10:45.

55 John 8:34.

56 Mark 12:30-31.

57 Luke 24:36-43 and John 21:12-13.

58 John 11:25-26 and Philippians 3:21.

59 Revelation 21:5.

60 See Romans 8:18-23 and Revelation 21–22.

Chapter 6

61 Acts 2:22-37.

62 Acts 2:38.

63 Matthew 16:24 and John 10:10.

64 Psalm 113.

65 Acts 2:42.

66 1 Corinthians 15:20-57.

67 1 Corinthians 15:58.

Conclusion

68 John 11:25; John 10:10-15; Luke 9:23.

Appendices

69 Paul Davies, "Physics and the Mind of God: The Templeton Prize Address", 1995: www.scribd.com/document/486238218/Davies-Physics-and-the-Mind-of-God-FT-doc (accessed 10 Jun. 2025).

70 Albert Einstein, "Science and Religion" (*Nature*, Vol. 146, 9 Nov. 1940, p. 605-607): www.nature.com/articles/146605a0.pdf (accessed 23 Oct. 2018).

71 John Polkinghorne, *Reason and Reality* (SPCK, 1991), p. 76.

72 "Letter to William Graham, 3rd July 1881". The University of Cambridge Darwin Correspondence Project: www.darwinproject.ac.uk/letter?docId=letters/DCP-LETT-13230.xml (accessed 28 Jun. 2018).

73 John Polkinghorne, *One World* (SPCK, 1986), p. 92.

74 Thomas Nagel, *Mind and Cosmos* (OUP, 2012), p. 14.

75 C.S. Lewis, *Miracles* (Touchstone, 1996), p. 23.

76 John 14:6.

77 Acts 4:12.

78 Colossians 1:15.

79 John 14:9.

80 John 5:18; 20:28.

ACKNOWLEDGEMENTS

Like the rest of life with Jesus, writing this book has been a team effort. I couldn't have done it alone and I wouldn't have wanted to. First, I am so thankful to Rachael, my life-long teammate, not just for her unrelenting support and encouragement but for the profound ways in which God has been using her to make me more like Jesus for the last 14 years, and through that making this book a lot better than it ever could have been without her.

Second, I am so grateful for Katy Morgan, who has brilliantly championed and shaped this book from the earliest stages. She is both a good friend and a truly gifted editor, and this book is definitely the result of a creative collaboration between us—it really feels like her name ought to be on the cover as well.

Sincere thanks also to everyone who kindly read through earlier drafts and gave me feedback. Alice, Steve, Motsy, Adam, Pete, Matt, Ed, Andy, Andy, Mum and Dad, I really appreciate it. Your comments were hugely helpful.

I am also indebted to the wonderful people who shared their stories with me and the difference the resurrection of Jesus makes to them for the final two chapters. It was gutting not to be able to include something from each of you but I was deeply encouraged and helped by what everyone shared—so a massive thank you to Rhydhm, Naushin, Jan, Claire, Alex, Anna, Tim, Joanna, Alison, Chris, Tia, Rob, Ellie, Margaret, Chia-Wen, Shirley and André.

Finally I want to thank my church family at Eden Baptist Church. Over these last few years, God has shown so much of his care and kindness to me through you, and done so much of his work on me through you as well. I'm also very grateful for your generosity in giving me the time and encouragement to work on this—with special thanks to Julian, Graham and John.

KEEP EXPLORING YOUR SENSE OF MORE

Most of us have a sense that there may be more out there than only what we can see or touch—not necessarily a God but *something*. Through Luke Cawley's imaginative and thoughtful writing, discover the possibility that your sense of *something* correlates to a *someone* who not only exists but can be encountered and known in the person of Jesus.

DO SCIENCE AND RELGION MIX?

Many today see no need or use for belief systems that offer answers to the mysteries of our universe. Science has explained it, they assume. Religion is redundant. But Oxford Maths Professor John Lennox offers a fresh way of thinking about science and Christianity—revealing that not only are they not opposed, but they can and must mix to give us a fuller understanding of the universe and the meaning of existence.

thegoodbook.com/can-science-explain-everything

thegoodbook.co.uk/can-science-explain-everything

thegoodbook.com.au/can-science-explain-everything

BIBLICAL | RELEVANT | ACCESSIBLE

At The Good Book Company we are dedicated to helping Christians and local churches grow. We believe that God's growth process always starts with hearing clearly what he has said to us through his timeless and flawless word—the Bible.

Ever since we opened our doors in 1991, we have been striving to produce resources that are biblical, relevant, and accessible. By God's grace, we have grown to become an international publisher, encouraging ordinary Christians of every age and stage and every background and denomination to live for Christ day by day and equipping churches to grow in their knowledge of God, their love for one another, and the effectiveness of their outreach.

Call one of our friendly team for a discussion of your needs or visit one of our local websites for more information on the resources and services we provide.

Your friends at The Good Book Company